MUKWAHEPO
woman soldier mother

As told to **Ellen Ndeshi Namhila**

UNAM PRESS
UNIVERSITY OF NAMIBIA

University of Namibia Press
Private Bag 13301
Windhoek
Namibia
www.unam.na
unampress@unam.na

© Ellen Ndeshi Namhila, 2013

All rights reserved. No part of this publication may be reproduced, stored in any retrieval system or transmitted in any form, or by any means, e.g. electronic, mechanical, photocopying, recording or otherwise without prior permission of the author.

First published: 2013
Design and layout: Silke Kotze
Cover design and illustrations: Romeo Sinkala
Printed by: John Meinert Printers, Windhoek

ISBN: 978-99916-42-19-2

Distribution:
In Namibia by Demasius Publications:
www.demasius-publications.com
Internationally by the African Books Collective:
www.africanbookscollective.com

CONTENTS

Introduction v

Map xiii

Woman
1 Life-changing Words 1
2 The Journey into Exile 9

Soldier
3 Military Training in Kongwa 31

Mother
4 Zambia 61
5 Angola 81
6 The Coming of Independence 99

Mukwahepo
7 Returning Home 113
8 Life in Independent Namibia 129

About the Author 141

Acknowledgements 141

INTRODUCTION

by Ellen Ndeshi Namhila

We arrived in Nyango, a SWAPO[1] camp in Zambia, in August 1978. We were a group of fifteen girls. All of us were survivors of the Cassinga massacre. Cassinga was a SWAPO refugee camp in Angola, which was bombed by the South African Defence Force on 4 May 1978. Following our evacuation from the devastated camp, SWAPO embarked on a vigorous campaign to find scholarships that would allow many of its young people an opportunity to study in other African countries, as well as in Cuba. The fifteen of us were interviewed by two people from the Commonwealth. We were then sent to Nyango, from where we expected to proceed to West Africa to complete our secondary education.

In Nyango, we were immediately integrated with other Namibian students. One day, a group of us were sitting in the shade of a tree near the communal kitchen. We saw a small crowd walking very quickly towards us from a distance. 'It is *Meekulu*[2] Mukwahepo,'[3] one of the girls shouted. As the crowd advanced towards us, I saw about eight children walking in front of a beautiful woman wearing an African print dress. In my mind I assumed they were Zambians crossing through our camp to their homes because this had often happened in Angola, from where I had just come. As they came closer to us, one of us said, '*Walelepoo, meeku,*' (Good afternoon, grandmother). The crowd stopped suddenly

---

1   SWAPO (South West Africa People's Organisation) is a national liberation movement that was formed in 1960. Its pledge was to unite the Namibian people in a mass-based organisation dedicated to national independence. The common experience of colonial oppression united Namibians from different language groups to forge political unity under SWAPO.
2   *Meekulu* means grandmother. It comes from the words *mee* (mother) and *kulu* (literally senior, but in English it is translated 'grand'), therefore grandmother.
3   *Mukwanangobe* is an Oshiwambo noun, which comes from the word *mukwa* meaning 'belonging to' and *nangobe* meaning 'cattle'. Traditionally, every child born in an Owambo family has two family totems to which he or she belongs, one denoting the paternal and the other the maternal clan. Mukwanangobe (her paternal totem) means 'one who belongs to the cattle clan'. Mukwahepo means 'one who belongs to the poor clan', *hepo* coming from the word *oluhepo*, which means 'poverty'. Although every child has two totem names, only women are affectionately called by these totems, and always by the paternal totem, never by the maternal one. Mukwahepo is neither the maternal nor the paternal totem of Mukwahepo's, but rather one that was placed upon her by her peers during military training in Kongwa, Tanzania.

and the woman said, 'Good afternoon, children, and what are you doing under the tree?'

'We are playing games.'

'Ok, have fun,' she said.

She waved at us and walked on. We saw a cloud of dust left behind by Mukwahepo and her children as they disappeared from sight down the sand path.

I was impressed by the woman and her children. They gave me the feeling of a family with a purpose. I inquired from our colleagues in Nyango about who Mukwahepo was. 'Oh, you do not know who Mukwahepo is? My goodness, she is the first Namibian woman who went into exile. She was the only woman amongst thousands of men.'

'What about all those children with her, whose are they as they all seemed to be around the same age?' I asked.

'They are her children, she has lots of kids and she lives with them in a big house over there. Mukwahepo is a very important figure here in this camp. When our most important leaders visit Nyango, they all go to greet Mukwahepo at her home. They have to go to her, you understand! She is one of those who were cooked in big pots in Tanzania.' I did not ask any more questions out of fear of being seen to be ignorant. I left Nyango camp in September 1979 and went to The Gambia, West Africa, with this mental picture of Mukwahepo.

I completed my secondary education in The Gambia in 1983 and returned to Angola. I was assigned to teach Namibian children at the primary school in the province of Kwanza-Sul. Unlike Nyango camp in Zambia, the camp at Kwanza-Sul was huge. I settled in an area called Lukunga. I do not know why I chose to settle there, as Lukunga was inhabited by school-going young boys and a few male teachers.

It did not take me long to realise that the very same Mukwahepo, whom I had briefly encountered in Zambia, lived in the neighbourhood. I walked past her house every day to and from school but never tried to approach her to announce my presence, or just to greet her. There were often people, especially women and children, sitting outside her home. I used to greet them and walk on. I had the idea that Mukwahepo had so many children because she was the first Namibian woman to join SWAPO in exile and therefore had to reproduce and 'reconstruct' Namibia in exile.

One day, I returned from school to find two colleagues seated under the tree in front of my home. When I joined them, they told me that they were waiting to see Mukwahepo. Sitting under the tree overlooking her house would enable them to spot her when she arrived home. My interest was again awoken. 'Can you visit Mukwahepo in this manner?' I asked.

'Yes, of course, everybody does it. You mean to say that you have never been to her place?' one of them replied.

'Never,' I said.

'Shame, what is your problem?' she asked. I did not reply. I had just thought that it was disrespectful to simply walk over to see Mukwahepo when I had nothing to say to her.

When they saw Mukwahepo approaching, they stood up and walked over to her house, and I joined them. Mukwahepo is naturally a very happy person so she welcomed us all as if she had known us for a thousand years. Her children came to greet us, then left. 'Good afternoon, teacher,' they greeted, showing their respect for me. One of my colleagues, Theresia, told Mukwahepo that the school principal had told her to leave for Luanda with the next convoy. She had received a scholarship to study in the United Kingdom for two years, and she wished to leave her eighteen-month-old baby girl under the care of Mukwahepo. 'The house is full to capacity, as you can see for yourself, but if you truly wish to leave your baby with me, I will do my best to take care of her,' said Mukwahepo with a smile. 'Bring your baby here, my child. Go and study hard. I will gladly look after your baby.'

Problem solved, and we left Mukwahepo's house. I asked Theresia how long she had known Mukwahepo. 'I do not know her personally,' she said.

'Then how can you leave your child with her?' I asked.

'She is our *meme* (mother) and she loves children. I have seen people leaving their children with their age-mates, but then the child is passed on to someone else when that person leaves Luanda to go to school somewhere else. Children do not respond well when they are continually passed from one caretaker to another. I will have peace of mind if I leave my baby with Mukwahepo because I know I will find her under Mukwahepo's care when I return from school,' she explained. I now understood how Mukwahepo acquired her children and also understood a bit more about her personality.

In 1985, I left Kwanza-Sul and went to study in Finland. I did not hear about Mukwahepo again until 1997, when her name was mentioned in conversation. It was said that she was devastated by the loss of one of her exile children. I thought that I would make her the offer of coming to stay with me in Windhoek for a while, to give her an opportunity to reflect, accept and start healing. I traced her through the SWAPO office in Oshikango and made her this offer in the spirit of comradeship and solidarity, which was shared by all Namibians in exile. I felt obliged to help one of our comrades to recover from her loss. I also made the offer due to my own experience, as my husband had died on 1 March 1990, only three weeks before the independence of Namibia, on 21 March. He died because of the excitement of Namibian independence. My comrades were celebrating the independence of our country while I was mourning my husband. At the same time that I was excited about the independence that for such a long time we had yearned for, I was faced with the death of my husband. I was devastated. I felt lonely and abandoned. I wanted to show solidarity with Mukwahepo because I knew the deep pain of having lost someone close. Sadly, Mukwahepo's visit did not work out well.

She arrived on the weekend, which gave us time to show her around our house and explain how things worked. On Monday, when I got up to prepare to go to work, Mukwahepo was already up and dressed. I wondered whether she was coming with me to work. I casually told her that she did not need to get up so early, that she needed to rest. I thought she had understood me, but the next morning she did the same thing. She got up and asked for work. I did not know what to do because I did not have any work for her. So I left her at home with the children and our house helper.

When I arrived home from work, Mukwahepo had many questions. She wanted to know who our neighbours were. But I did not know any of our neighbours. The next day, she decided to take our children for a walk and narrowly escaped a vicious dog attack on our street. She was frightened by this experience. My head was spinning. I could not understand how a person whom I thought I was helping was turning all the efforts I was making on her behalf on their head. I began to question my decision to invite her to stay.

Mukwahepo was an elderly woman. As I was a lot younger than her, I thought that this might be causing a barrier between us and making her feel uncomfortable. I therefore decided to rethink my approach. It was becoming clear to me that Mukwahepo had her expectations, just as I had mine. We did not have a common understanding as to how her visit could benefit her most. I started to ask myself what I knew about Mukwahepo. The answer was simple. I did not know her at all. Everything I knew about her was based on second-hand knowledge that was passed from mouth to ear. I had never questioned the validity of such information or the integrity of the sources from which it came. I had rushed into bringing her to Windhoek without considering these issues. It was not working out because maybe Mukwahepo was not the person whom I had been told she was.

I decided to ask her to tell me who she really was, what kind of life she had led during the struggle, and what had happened to her after independence. I thought that knowing her historical background – her story – would put me in a better position to give her support, even if only in a small way. She agreed.

In the evenings after work, Mukwahepo and I sat down on the *stoep* (veranda) at the back of my house and she narrated her life story to me. This story-telling soon became a routine for us and we both enjoyed the experience. I wrote down what I considered important in my notebook. I was captivated by her life story, which she narrated in a soft tone of voice, remaining calm even whilst describing life-threatening events.

I realised that Mukwahepo was naturally a very happy person. She had led a busy life, surrounded by people all the time. She was not used to sitting around doing nothing; she enjoyed keeping busy. I realised that things would have worked out differently if I had given her work to do. Mukwahepo wanted to be surrounded by people, but I had left her at home and gone to work. And our social environment in Windhoek was not as welcoming and open as the environment she was used to, so she did not feel at home.

One day, Mukwahepo asked me for a lift to the SWAPO office in Windhoek. I took her there in the morning and went to work. I was happy that she would probably meet some of her comrades. When I picked her up at lunchtime, I felt that her problem had worsened. She said that the comrades were too busy and did not have time to talk or listen to her. She felt that some of them whom she had known quite well in exile were avoiding talking to her. I shared my experience with her, telling her that on some days I am so busy that it is not always possible to see a person who just arrives without an appointment. This made sense to her, and she agreed that next time we should make an appointment.

The next day, I took her with me to the National Assembly where I worked. When I got too busy with something that required peace and quiet, I sent her to the cafeteria. Mukwahepo loves cakes, so she went happily. I suggested too that she walk in the foyer and corridors of the building, and in the beautiful surrounding park. This resulted in her being noticed by some of her former comrades who had become Members of Parliament. The Namibian President, Comrade Sam Nujoma, heard that Mukwahepo was around and invited her to State House. She also received a formal invitation to visit the SWAPO headquarters. Some of the parents of children whom Mukwahepo had raised at Old Farm[4] and in Nyango heard about her visit. They invited her to their homes for dinner and bought her nice clothes. The Muteka family, for example, had her stay for a whole week so that she could also see the children. Mukwahepo was so happy.

When she came back from the Muteka family, we continued with our story-telling. I was very captivated by her story and just continued to listen for days and days. What started as a story motivated by the need to understand Mukwahepo in order to provide her with humanitarian support, widened into the life story of an extraordinary woman. Mukwahepo educated me about the liberation struggle, and about life in general. I learnt from talking to her that it may not be fair to base our assessment of people on second-hand information, as many stories I had heard about Mukwahepo had no basis in fact. I had lived about a

---

4   A SWAPO camp in Lusaka, Zambia (see later in the story).

hundred metres from her house in Kwanza-Sul from 1983 to 1985, yet realised that I had not known her at all.

Namibian society is strongly rooted in oral history. Most of what we know about our past is not documented. The history of our liberation struggle is no exception. This history is threatened by the advanced age of most of the veterans of the struggle. Many have already passed away, their memories untapped. There is an urgency to record the stories of those who are still alive. Speaking from experience, I completed the biography of Kaxumba kaNdola[5] by piecing together information from interviews with his family, friends, enemies, former prison inmates and political activists. He died in 1997 after my first interview with him. Two of the five women who are the subject of my latest book[6] have also passed away. One died before the book was published; the other soon after the book was launched.

My decision to write this book about Mukwahepo was based on the observation that there is a lack of literature about the liberation struggle. The little that does exist focuses on men and hardly acknowledges the contributions made by women in the struggle. While the story of Mukwahepo can hardly fill this huge gap, it can contribute significantly to this history. She presents unique experiences of women in the struggle. And it is this uniqueness of her own life story that makes her exceptional. I am glad she gave me permission to write her story.

I used Mukwahepo's story to develop themes in this book, such as childhood and family roots. I thought carefully about what questions I wanted her to answer for each theme, and prepared a list of questions. Then, in 2003, with this list of questions, a tape recorder, a notebook and a camera, I went to interview her. I later expanded some of the themes into the chapters of this book.

When I had sat down with Mukwahepo in the informal setting of my home, she had spoken openly. There was a flow of events in her story and I felt that she had enjoyed telling me about her life. Yet when I went to interview her formally in 2003, with a tape recorder in my hands,

---

5   Namhila, E.N. (2005): *Kaxumba KaNdola: Man and Myth. The Biography of a Barefoot Soldier.* Basel: Basler Afrika Bibliographien. ISBN: 3-905141-86-8.
6   Namhila, E.N. (2009): *Tears of Courage: Five Mothers, Five Stories, One Victory.* Windhoek: AACRLS. ISBN: 978-99916-44-12-7.

the passion of story-telling was lost. She was very tense and I had to constantly probe – something I did not do when she had narrated her story to me at my home. I assume that she did not respond well to being recorded. She spoke very slowly, with long pauses between her words. I felt that maybe she did not trust me any longer with her information, or perhaps would have preferred just talking to me without the tape recorder. I suggested that we stop the interview, to which she agreed. Then, in 2004, I paid her a surprise visit. I brought up the subject of our interviews, and she laughed and asked me where her book was. So we resumed the interviews, but this time without the tape recorder. All I had was a list of questions and a notebook. Mukwahepo began to talk freely, and the tension was gone. This was how I interviewed her from then on.

Once the interviews were over, I began to write down the story, comparing the text from the discussions with that from the interviews. I modified the questions and rescheduled another interview with her in 2006. I informed her that I would bring a tape recorder, and she agreed. I recorded another follow-up interview in 2009, which included general questions to cover issues that she considered outstanding, funny, regrettable or meaningful at various stages in her life. The recordings were then transcribed and translated from Oshiwambo into English, and integrated into the story. I interviewed her for the last time in 2012 after the manuscript was reviewed.

I interviewed Mukwahepo five times over a period of fifteen years.[7] Having carried her story for sixteen years, I now feel it is time to let it out. This book narrates the story of Mukwahepo as a young woman journeying into exile, joining the armed liberation struggle there, the different roles she played in exile during the struggle, and what became of her after she returned to Namibia for the coming of independence.

Windhoek, 2013

---

7 Both my interview notes and the tapes are deposited at the National Archives of Namibia.

Southern Africa

WOMAN

1
LIFE-CHANGING WORDS

'I have come to collect you. I want you to pack your bag so we can leave right now, tonight, this moment. I will explain to you later where we are going. But it is a long journey that I cannot take without you.' These words, spoken by my fiancé, Shikongo shaHangala, changed my life completely. They marked the starting point of an arduous and testing physical, emotional and psychological journey; a journey that transformed me from a shy, traditional Owambo village girl to a national hero; a mother of the struggle for the freedom and independence of Namibia.

On that fateful Saturday in March 1963, I had joined my aunt and some other women in the neighbouring homestead to perform *ekolo*.[8] While we were busy harvesting, a child came running to find us. She was sent to fetch me because there were important visitors at our home who were urgently asking to see me. The child did not give any details about who the visitors were or why they had not come to the harvesting site to find me. Bewildered, I left my harvesting duties and headed home, where I found two men waiting for me.

The men informed me that they had come from Ongandjera. Shikongo shaHangala had sent them to tell me that he was about to undertake a very important and urgent mission, and wanted me to prepare myself for this journey with him because he would not go without me. He would come later in the evening to fetch me and wanted to find me ready for the journey. They warned me not to tell a soul about the mission.

---

8   *Ekolo* is the harvesting of ripe marula fruits and is a very important cultural activity in our culture. It is always carried out in groups of women and girls, and every girl child has to learn to master it from early childhood. The process is done very fast, and a talented woman can process more than six fruits per minute. *Ekolo* brings village women together to exchange news and views, and to advise each other on matters affecting their lives in the community.

As I returned to my task of harvesting marula, I wondered why my fiancé wanted me to go along with him, and how long the journey would take. As soon as we had finished, I rushed home, packed my belongings quickly, and continued with my usual household chores of cooking dinner for my family. I also informed my aunt and uncle that Shikongo would be visiting us that evening.

I expected Shikongo to arrive in a respectable manner that was acceptable to my parents and I. When he eventually did arrive, however, he came embarrassingly late. He offered his apology, and my parents accepted his explanation because he had walked a very long distance from Ongandjera to Onengali yaKaluvi in Oukwanyama. In those days, it was difficult to get a lift as very few people owned cars. Shikongo was allowed to visit me and to spend an evening or night with me at least once or twice a year.

According to traditional culture, when a couple were engaged and slept in the same bed, the boy was to sleep with his clothes on so that the next morning his body and clothes would be red from the ochre dye that had been applied to the girl's body. This was proof that he had spent the night with her. The boy would then spend several days in those clothes to demonstrate to the world that his fiancée was a traditional girl, and for everyone to know that he had visited her. The boy would feel great pride to show that his fiancée was a girl of culture and tradition. If the girl's parents failed to cover their daughter well with dye, and the following day the boy had no dye on him, it was considered a big social shame to the girl's family, and a public humiliation for the boy. The boy then had the customary right to dump the girl, who was considered scandalous. If a boy and girl were engaged, and both sets of parents recognised their engagement, they were allowed to spend time together, although they had to obey certain rules. They were allowed to caress each other but only when they were alone in the girl's room, and usually when it was dark, but they were not allowed to hold hands or kiss in public. They were also not allowed to have intercourse. If they did, and the girl fell pregnant, both of them would be disgraced through public burning until death. Every young person knew that pregnancy before marriage was a taboo and a capital offence.

I came from a family that had been converted to Christianity during the early encounters with missionaries. I was therefore not cleansed and oiled like girls from non-Christian homes. Christian girls did not go through the oiling practice because the Church disapproved of sleepover visits.

If the boy was coming to spend the night, the custom was that he should arrive at least before sunset, or before the cattle returned from grazing. It was considered extremely disrespectful for a prospective son-in-law to enter the house after this time. If this happened, the father of the girl had the right to chase the scandalous boy away and bar him from marrying his daughter. Usually, the boy initiated the visit by informing his parents, who in turn would send a messenger to ask permission from the girl's parents, at least a week in advance, so that they could prepare their daughter both physically and psychologically for his visit.

In Christian families, when a boy slept over at his future father-in-law's house, he was obliged to wake up in the morning earlier than everyone else in the household and start working in the field, milking the cows or mending the fences. This was to show his male talents to the girl's family and the whole community. The father-in-law and brother-in-laws would accompany him so as to study his work ethics and his manly manners, and to assess whether he was a man capable of being entrusted with their daughter or sister. During the day, even the neighbours would come to observe and evaluate the worthiness of his work and to ask him questions. The father-in-law may have asked his future son-in-law to build him a hut, not necessarily because he needed a hut, but simply to evaluate his skills. The son-in-law would begin to design the base and put up the structure under the watchful eyes of his in-laws, who would also actively engage him in conversation. They would even offer him food, to test whether he would compromise work for food; whether he would leave work unfinished to go and eat. This social conduct allowed the girl's family to study the personality of the boy. The boy knew that he would be watched and tested; his parents would have prepared him psychologically to go through these community assessments of his worthiness as a man.

The girl was also allowed to have a sleepover visit at her fiancé's house, but she was usually accompanied by two or three of her best girlfriends. She too was subjected to rigorous observation by her prospective in-laws. The girl had to wake up very early in the morning to pound mahangu into flour, a task she was expected to accomplish before sunrise. Later in the morning, she was expected to go into the fields to demonstrate her ability to till the land (*takupaula etemo*). Usually, parents would prepare their daughters well for such visits so that they did not disgrace their families and the people who had raised them. These kinds of interactions, although stressful for the young couples, were important socially. They also allowed couples to get to know one another before marriage. Engaged couples carefully selected the right friends to accompany them on such visits. The friends acted as advisors, timekeepers and bodyguards, and any mistake in choosing a friend could cost a girl or boy their marriage.

According to our culture, I was no longer considered a girl because, from the day my family had put me through the traditional wedding transitional rites, I was considered a woman. So, on that Saturday in March when Shikongo arrived at my home, he was served some traditional food, and as soon as he had finished eating, the people in our home went to bed, leaving us alone to discuss things.

I was eager to find out what Shikongo had in mind, but he waited until the whole household was quiet. It was then that he said those fateful words that changed my life forever; that he had come to collect me to go on a long journey with him that he could not undertake without me. He told me that we were going to meet some of his friends at Oshikango, and that from there we would continue our journey into Angola.

It is difficult to tell you why I followed Shikongo shaHangala, especially as I did not even know the place we were going to. I loved Shikongo. He was my fiancé and I trusted him. I felt that he would not take me anywhere unless he was sure that the place we were going to was safe and would meet the approval of my parents. And so, with this faith and trust, and a bag containing my few belongings, I embarked on an eventful and dangerous journey that would take me through

Cabinda (a province of Angola), the Congo[9], Northern Rhodesia[10] and Nyasaland[11] to Tanganyika.[12] I also had no idea that I was making history by becoming the first Namibian woman to cross the border into exile to join SWAPO.

* * * * * *

But before I tell that story, I should explain a little about myself.

I was born Mukwanangobe Aguste yaImmanuel, the daughter of Immanuel Haipinge and Antonia Ndemweetela yaMwalondange. I come from a very small family with a complicated history. I am the last-born of my parents' three children. My father, Immanuel Haipinge, was an only child, and nothing is known about whether he had any brothers or sisters whom he had not met. The only relative we knew from my father's family was his uncle, Haimini yaHalweendo. The relationship between my father and uncle Haimini was also never explained, even though when I was growing up I felt the very close relationship they must have had. I find it sad that this relationship was not explained to us because it is very important for me to know how I relate to people. However, I have grown with it and accepted this reality.

The maternal side of my family has its roots in Kaoko. One thing I vividly recall is my grandmother reminding us from time to time that '*fye Ovashimba va Kaoko*' (we are Ovashimba from Kaoko). As a child, the tonation of the '*shimba*', '*themba*' or '*himba*' did not really matter to me because in my mind it referred to the same thing. You (rightfully) asked me today whether I descend from the Ovatjimba, Ovazemba or Ovahimba. My answer is that my forbearers are now not here to clarify this matter, but I initially understood it to mean Ovazemba from Kaoko.

My mother, Antonia Ndemweetela yaMwalondange, was the daughter of an Ovazemba woman from Kaoko. Both my great-grandparents are Ovazemba from Kaoko, who migrated to Ongandjera

---

9   The Congo became Zaire in 1971 and was renamed The Democratic Republic of the Congo (DRC) in 1997. Mukwahepo refers to it as the Congo.
10 Northern Rhodesia was renamed Zambia after independence in 1964.
11 Nyasaland was renamed Malawi after independence in 1964.
12 Tanganyika and Zanzibar united in 1964 to form the United Republic of Tanganyika and Zanzibar, which later the same year was renamed Tanzania.

with their two children, a boy named Malenga (Namalenga) and a girl named Sofia shaMungoloka, my grandmother. Mungoloka, our great-grandfather, was apparently a very rich man. He possessed a lot of cattle. I can still remember how my mother used to talk about him and his wealth, especially his cattle.

My grandmother, Sofia shaMungoloka, also known by her totem name, Mukwanambwa gwaNgoloka, married Tshikesho from Uukwambi. She left her family in Ongandjera to settle in Uukwambi. In this marriage, she was blessed with three children – two boys, Tshaduka and Meneta, and one girl, Sofia. Their father, Tshikesho, passed away, and in those days there was no law to protect women and their children after the death of a husband. The security for most women was in marriage. So my grandmother remarried Mwalondange yaHashipala and settled at Eenhana daMwoongela village in Oukwanyama. My mother, Antonia Ndemweetela yaMwalondange, was born out of this marriage. My mother grew up and married Immanuel Haipinge, my father. They settled at a village called Onengali yaKaluvi where my brother, Rafael, my sister, Maria, and I were born.

I was born on 7 October 1937, the youngest in my family. Our father died very young, probably in his late thirties, leaving my mother to fend for the family. When he died, us children were still young. I was still a baby so have no memory of him at all. As my mother was still breastfeeding me, the headman of Onengali yaKaluvi village allowed her to continue living in my father's homestead for eighteen months. Apparently, it was a taboo to chase a woman away from her deceased husband's homestead if she was breastfeeding a baby. However, my mother and her children were ordered to vacate my father's homestead as soon as the headman realised that she had stopped breastfeeding me. I therefore kept my family in their homestead for nearly two years after my father's death.

The land-use right to my father's homestead was sold to another community member and my mother had to find another place to live and raise her children. So she packed all her belongings and moved to the house of her brother, Meneta haTshikesho, where she and my brother and sister took refuge for a while. Life was not easy for my family, and there was a time when my mother had offered to take us with her to Ongandjera to her mother's brother, our great-uncle, Namalenga, so that he could give us some cattle. As children, we were not interested in the idea of our mother taking us to Ongandjera to meet our relatives. Now that I am an adult, I regret not having accepted her offer. I do not have a strong family network, as my brother and sister have both passed away and the only relatives I have are my sister's daughter and her children. Now that I realise the importance of the connection to our relatives in Ongandjera, our mother is deceased and the opportunity is gone. We have lost our maternal roots and do not know how to trace them. We do not know what village in Ongandjera to trace Namalenga yaMungoloka because all the people of that line are dead and have left no word of their roots. We were children and did not realise the significance of our family history. Now we are lost. We cannot find our way back to our past.

Following the death of my father, and after we had to leave his homestead, my paternal uncle, Haimini yaHalweendo, inherited me. Unfortunately, my mother, brother and sister did not really have a welcoming family to shelter them. Uncle Haimini was a gatherer and unifier of people. He and his wife were kind-hearted people who had the special talent of keeping the family together. Later, he established an enclosure for my mother and invited her and her children to come and live at his homestead. This is where my mother lived until the end of her life.

******

I was brought up under the care of my uncle, Haimini, who raised me as a Christian. Then, in 1954, the very same elders who had brought me up as a Christian decided to put me through a traditional marriage transitional rite (*meengoma*). My family married me off to Nakale kaHangula yaKangudo, the son of Mweshiininga shaMbishi. Mweshiininga was the daughter of Mbishi, a prominent member of the Kwanyama royal family. This was a polygamous marriage and I was not prepared for it. It was not easy being married at the age of seventeen and being a member of the royal family. Nakale was an older man, and the senior wives were my mother's age and were much more experienced than I was. I was afraid, and too young to understand what marriage was all about. If there had been somewhere to go, I would have run away from the marriage. If I had had a protector, I would have called on him or her. But there was no such place or person, and so I obeyed my elders and suffocated in the marriage. After two years of misery, my family came to take me away and I returned to my uncle's house. Although I was still under twenty years old, I was considered to be a divorced woman.

******

I was visiting my sister at Ohakweenyanga village near Ongwediva in 1962 when I met Shikongo shaHangala, who could not take his eyes off me. He proposed marriage and we got engaged. Although women are not supposed to show affection, I was deeply in love with Shikongo. I expected to marry him, have children and be surrounded by my family. But Shikongo had other ideas. In 1963, he took me on the long journey into exile. This journey was so dramatic that even Shikongo was weighed down by the turn of events. It is this journey that changed my life forever.

2
THE JOURNEY INTO EXILE

When everyone in the house was fast asleep, Shikongo and I hit the road, en route to Angola. We walked to a house in Oshikango, where we found Filimon Andreas (Kashabubu), Johannes yaHaukongo (Danger) and Filipus Haukongo waiting for us. We rested for a while and as soon as *mawila* (the morning star) rose in the east, we were all on our feet. We walked on and on the whole day up to Ondjiva. Shikongo knew that my sister was living in Ondjiva. He asked whether we could stay at her house, which we did for three weeks. From the time of our arrival in Ondjiva, Shikongo and his comrades were restless. They left my sister's house every single day before sunrise and returned very late in the evening. They went to town, but I had no idea what they were looking for.

While we were in Ondjiva, I noticed that Shikongo had a lot of money. His purse was full of South African rands. He gave all this currency to me to take care of, and every morning when he left the house he took a big bundle of it with him. On his return in the evenings, he brought back even bigger bundles of Angolan (or rather Portuguese) escudos. He also gave this to me for safekeeping. This happened every day until all the South African currency that he had brought from Namibia was exchanged for Angolan money. I had no idea where he exchanged the money, with whom and why, but I did my best to keep our money safe. He also bought food for my sister and I to cook for the whole household.

******

We stayed in Ondjiva for three weeks. One day, Shikongo told me that we would be continuing with our journey the following day, and by morning we were again on our feet. We left Ondjiva for Luanda in a vehicle driven by a Portuguese man. It was during this journey that I realised the importance of the currencies we had acquired, which we used to pay for the services of this man and his private vehicle. With this money, we also bought food to sustain ourselves during the journey to Luanda.

We set off from Ondjiva and drove up to Matala, a small mining town which later became home to many Namibian women and children. However, about three kilometres into the town, the driver stopped the lorry and asked us to disembark. He explained to us that twenty-four hour police checkpoints were set up on every road leading to or from Matala. He said that the police thoroughly searched the contents and people in every vehicle at these checkpoints. He pointed out to us that we might face problems at the checkpoints because we did not have all the required identification documents or residence permits to live in or travel through Angola. We too did not want to get arrested as illegal immigrants, and accepted his advice.

The Portuguese man advised us to look for the footpath alongside the tarred road toward Matala. He said we should follow that path until we reach the centre of town. Once in Matala, we should find our way to the exit road towards Luanda, and follow the footpaths until we saw his lorry after the police checkpoint. He advised us to take only our critical essentials and leave the rest of our belongings in the vehicle. It was difficult to trust a stranger, but we had no alternative. Luckily, the man was honest, and after about three hours of walking we found him and his lorry waiting for us outside the town. We were happy. He bought food and drinks for us and offered to drive us to a place where we cooked the food. We ate well and continued our journey.

I was surprised that during our journey I was not allowed to cook. It was the men who prepared the food. I just sat and watched, waiting to be served. This was indeed a privilege. Apparently, it was a taboo for a woman to cook if she was alone with men in the forest. During our meals, I was always the last one to finish eating. I was not allowed to stop eating even when my stomach was full because this was apparently also a taboo. I therefore had to continue eating small portions slowly until all the men had finished, so that I would always finish last.

Our journey from Ondjiva to Luanda took us nearly five days of driving. It was during this journey that Shikongo told me where we were actually going. He said that we were en route to Tanganyika, where many other exiled Namibians went to pursue the liberation of our country. He told me that we were going to seek the support of the United Nations (UN), which would enable us to return home fully prepared to rid our country of the colonisers so that we could be free. He also warned me that if anyone asked who we were and where we were going, I had to say that we were South West Africans going to work at the coffee plantations in Angola. This is what he apparently told the Portuguese man who was driving us to Luanda.

******

We arrived in Luanda five days after leaving Ondjiva. The Portuguese man helped to arrange our transport from Luanda to Nambuangongo before he returned to Ondjiva. We stayed in Luanda for about a week. I was fascinated with Luanda. I had never before seen anything like it, a huge and very beautiful city. The streets were full of smart-looking people (both black and white), constantly coming and going, looking very busy and sure of themselves. I was seeing beautiful black women with very long hair for the first time. I had never seen such huge buildings and so many cars – some moving, others stationary. I had never seen anything like Luanda and felt totally at a loss, and that I was the only one feeling that way. It was all like a magical dream. Soon we had to leave Luanda for Nambuangongo by minibus. I do not really know how this journey was organised, but Shikongo paid for all our expenses until we reached Nambuangongo. Here our luck shifted.

******

Nambuangongo was a town like any other. Its specific characteristics were that it was surrounded by very big farms, mainly cassava and coffee plantations. The huge coffee plantations which sustained the town were managed by the Portuguese, drawing on the manual labour of African workers. We stayed in Nambuangongo for about two weeks, and then the so-called War of the Panga broke out. This war was waged by Roberto Holden, the President of FNLA (Frente Nacional de Libertação de

Angola)[13] against the Portuguese colonial army and police, in response to the bombing of the township of Nambuangongo by these colonial forces.

One day, warplanes belonging to the Portuguese government in Angola suddenly zoomed in and started dropping petrol bombs on the township where the Angolan civilians lived. Everybody and everything became a target for the Caetano[14] military aggression. Although we were foreigners, we were indiscriminately bombed alongside the Angolan nationals. The FNLA soldiers came to rescue the local people by moving them away from the bombarded area into the forests.[15] We too started running. Even though we did not really understand what was going on, we realised the danger caused by the bombs and could see that if we did not run away like everyone else, the enemy bullets and petrol fires would annihilate us.

We ran for our lives as the Portuguese military planes continued to drop bombs on the township of Nambuangongo until they had burnt it to the ground. One of the advantages the Portuguese military had was that most of the Angolan houses were very susceptible to petrol bombs because they were constructed from materials that catch fire very quickly. It was therefore easy for them to set alight the whole township and burn everything to ashes.

The bombarded township of Nambuangongo consisted of the homes of the Angolan people of the town. The Portuguese settler community lived in town houses with their families, but many coffee plantation owners lived on their farms. The Angolan workers, the local population who were employed by the Portuguese farmers as casual farm labourers, established temporary shelters on the plantations, but their families lived in the township.

---

13 National Liberation Front of Angola.
14 Mukwahepo uses the word Caetano to mean the Portuguese colonial government of Angola, the colonial army and the police. Caetano was the Portuguese Prime Minister who succeeded Salazar in 1968 and ruled the colonies brutally. His harsh rule was so pervasive that his name could seemingly not be separated from the whole colonial system, including the police and the army, which was colloquially referred to as Caetano.
15 Actually, they were not real forests but the small bushes of the coffee plantations. For the sake of simplicity, they are referred to as forests in this text.

The population of Nambuangongo was large. There were thousands of people in the township. At that time, Angola was densely populated, unlike Namibia which had so few people. There were truly many people. I cannot guess a figure for you because we did not keep statistics and we were not counted by anyone. The only thing I can tell you is that very many people were displaced by the bombing.

The Angolan people hid in the forest while the Portuguese settlers joyfully occupied the whole town, celebrating their victory over the Angolan civilians. As soon as darkness fell over Nambuangongo, the FNLA freedom fighters launched the War of the Panga, retaliating against the Portuguese forces. The FNLA fighters hacked their enemy with pangas and axes, and Caetano suffered a total defeat because they seemingly did not expect this retaliation from the FNLA.

On the night of the attack, many Portuguese settlers fled the town of Nambuangongo, while a few held on until morning. They drove off leaving most of their belongings behind. Many went to settle in Luanda, apparently, and Nambuangongo became deserted. As soon as the Portuguese had left, the Angolans whose township had been bombed to ashes moved in and took over the town. However, before they could enjoy the comfort of the deserted town, Caetano's planes came back, this time bombing the town. They dropped bomb after bomb and destroyed the beautiful infrastructure of the town. When they were done with the town, the planes started dropping bombs on the coffee plantations in which we were hiding. This continuous bombardment created very big problems for the people because the bushes were short and did not really provide full cover. There were also a few big trees, but not enough to conceal everybody. The Caetano pilots realised the people would be in the big trees and started targeting them. Despite this, many of us survived the bombing without a single scratch.

While we were sheltering under cover of the coffee plantation, we had to observe very strict rules. For example, we were forbidden from making fires for warmth because if we lit fire, the enemy spy planes would see the smoke and attack us the next day. Or when we washed our clothes and hung them to dry on top of the bushes, or to allow the fresh air to blow over our blankets, these signals of our presence would also be picked up by the enemy. If we did not move away from the site immediately, Caetano would attack us the next day. The spy planes flew day and night. They did not make the same noisy sound as other warplanes. They made a sizzling noise. By the time we had heard these planes they had already done their spying work and were on their way out.

It was difficult to live in the forest, especially when Caetano intensified their attacks on us. The FNLA soldiers divided us up into two big groups in order to make it easier for logistics and to manage the security of the camp. The men were in one group while the women and children were in another. Being separated from Shikongo and the rest of my fellow Namibians frightened me. I feared being left alone with the Angolans because I did not have a common language with which to communicate with them or to understand what they were saying. I did not dare complain. I was afraid of what might happen to me if I had let the FNLA soldiers know that I was not an Angolan. War situations are complicated. So I kept quiet even though I was seriously worried about being separated from Shikongo and the others. I did not know where the FNLA soldiers had taken the men, or how long they would be gone. While we were in the forest of Nambuangongo, three other Oshiwambo-speaking Namibian men were brought to our camp. The FNLA soldiers had captured them from the farms where they had been working for Portuguese farmers.

These men, like all of us, did not like living in the forest, which was not out of choice but rather an emergency situation. Instead of being held up in the Angolan forest, they wanted to find their way back to Namibia. So they planned to escape from this FNLA-controlled camp. Early one morning, they succeeded in escaping from the camp, but by late afternoon they had been captured again by the FNLA and were returned to the camp. This time they were not put to live amongst us, but were isolated from us. We were informed that the people who had tried to escape from the camp had been caught, and that they would be punished. I do not know what eventually happened to them because we left them in this camp when we continued on our journey.

******

Staying in the Nambuangongo forest was not a matter of choice but a matter of survival. Even the Angolans with whom we were evacuated had no other way out because they had lost their livelihood. Their properties had been burnt down during the bombing. We had no food and medicine and we suffered from hunger and starvation. There was no food supply coming to us from anywhere and even when we had money in our pockets, it was of no use. We spent six months in the forest without eating any meat. I did not see any cattle or goats. Apart from snakes, there did not seem to be any wild animals. There were lots of snakes, the whole area was infested with them, but we Namibians do not eat snakes. The snakes were terrified by the bombs and by the humans. They did not bother anyone. As soon as they saw a human, they would slither away to hide somewhere far away. There were times when the people of Nambuangongo would go hunting, and return with a monkey and or a wild animal, called *kasheshe*. But Namibians do not believe in eating monkeys, and even if we had wanted to eat them, no one offered them to us.

For an entire six months we survived on stolen food. During the night, our male comrades left the camp in groups of five or six at a time to go into the nearby Portuguese farms to dig out cassava roots (*mazoka*). They would secretly enter the farm while the owners, their workers and their dogs were sleeping. And our men could not just walk freely into the farms of the Portuguese owners who had fled to Luanda, because there had been incidents where the Caetano soldiers had ambushed our people and attacked them on their way out of these deserted farms. These incidents had resulted in the loss of lives, as our people had been shot at close range. They did not have guns to defend themselves. It was actually after one such incident that our people came up with the strategy of going into a farm in groups of five or six at a time, and coming out in the same manner.

As soon as the men returned from the farms, the whole camp was called together to share whatever food they had brought. Each person in the camp was given a small piece of *mazoka* to eat. Us Namibians were not used to eating *mazoka*, raw *mazoka* for that matter, but we did not have a choice. We had to eat whatever was available or starve to death. It was difficult to secure food because the Caetano soldiers had a lot of information about the area and blocked all the routes to the food supply. Despite this possible danger, our men found a way to get through these obstacles, and on most days they brought us food. But there were days when there was no food at all. We trained our bodies to sleep for long hours in order to pass the time. This was how we survived for six months.

Like all the other men, Shikongo had to go on missions to search for food. I started worrying about the possibility of him being wounded or killed, because the men who went in search of food had no guarantee of returning unharmed and alive. It was wartime, and it was difficult to get information about people who went missing. You were lucky if, in the event of your husband disappearing, you were told what had become of him. I was happy that Shikongo always looked out for me during food distribution assembly. I appreciated that so much because it was the only opportunity we had to talk to each other and to know that we were both still alive and reasonably healthy. If a day or two passed without me seeing him, I got so worried that I became sick. I was more worried about Shikongo's safety than my own survival, maybe because I knew that my survival depended on him.

I was disturbed by the turn of events in Nambuangongo and worried about what I was going to do if something happened to Shikongo. I was scared. How was I going to survive on my own and find my way to Tanganyika? I felt helpless and did not want these thoughts to keep reappearing, but they did. I wished I was more prepared to meet the challenges of the journey. I did not want to believe that we were stuck in the coffee plantation. I was in this shocked state until the day that Shikongo came to look for me. He assured me that he would look after me and that, despite all these difficulties, we would reach Tanganyika. My hope was somehow restored.

The Nambuangongo coffee plantation was a very cold place. When the bombing had started that night, everyone was instructed to run away from the danger zone. There had been no time to run around to rescue our clothes or to pack our belongings. The blankets we had brought from home were burnt during the bombing. We ran away mainly with what we had on our bodies. I was fortunate because the attack found me wearing Shikongo's jacket and we had the chance to grab our bags with some clothes before we retreated.

Also, Nambuangongo was a very wet place; it rained and rained all the time. And with the wet weather came the cold. We were shivering and shaking from the cold all the time. This was very hard for me because it was also the first time I had spent nights, weeks and months in the forest away from my family and amongst people I did not know and with whom I had no common language. I also did not understand their culture. The only thing we had in common was our desire to stay alive, our struggle to survive.

There were also no health and medical facilities. We had no clinic, no nurses and no medicine to heal or cure people. When people got sick they either recovered naturally or they died. Small children got sick, very sick, and it broke my heart to just watch them suffer. Without medical help, the children often died. They died mainly from starvation, but illness and disease also greatly reduced their numbers.

The hunger did not only kill children; adults also died of starvation. I remember the owner of the house where we stayed in Nambuangongo. He too died in the forest, buried in the same manner as the others while we, the survivors, moved on. I did not really know him as it was Shikongo who had brought us to his house. I felt sad. Like everyone else who had died during this war, his final resting place just got lost because his grave was not marked with any symbol of remembrance. The family of the deceased would never know where their loved ones lay buried. Hunger, malaria and other ailments claimed their lives, and they would be lost forever without a trace.

There was one man who was injured during the bombing. He caught fire from the petrol bombs dropped by the Caetano planes and sustained burns all over his body. Even his hair was burnt from his head. His family and community carried him away from the fire and brought him into the forest, where he eventually died because there was no medical treatment to cure his burns. It pained me to glance at him and his wounds. When we first got to the camps in the forest he could somehow walk, but in the end his septic wounds became worse and worse until he could not even sit down anymore. It was a hopeless situation.

When people died, the others around them did the honour of giving them a decent burial. We normally erected a burial site, dug the grave, and buried the deceased quickly. After every death, the whole camp moved on to another site. At the place where the person was buried, there was no sign – no cross or symbol of remembrance – to say that so-and-so was buried here on such-and-such a date.

Amongst the people who escaped with us into the forest were Ovimbundu Angolans, of the Umbundu language group. One Ovimbundu woman lost her three children in this forest through starvation-related causes. The Angolans did not seem to practise herbal medicine. Even though we were in a forest full of herbs, the sick people were simply consumed by ailments, and many died, because their sickness was not treated. I knew that herbalism was not a profession that was usually practised in the open. However, I felt disappointed that none of the Angolans with us practised it even secretly. We had to watch helplessly as people were consumed by illness without being able to offer them any help. I felt bad to realise that I could not even help with a basic flu treatment.

******

Our journey into exile was eventful and challenging. The most fundamental challenge to us was that we could not communicate well in any of the local languages or in Portuguese, which was the lingua franca of Angola at that time. We could not easily express our thoughts or ask questions about issues affecting our survival. Also, we were travelling through Angola during a very difficult period of war and political uncertainty. We did not feel free to expose our identity because we feared that telling people that we were Namibians going to join SWAPO in Tanganyika would cause problems for us. We could not tell how FNLA would treat us or what they would do to us if they knew that we were Namibians.

Throughout our travels, our sympathisers often warned us to keep our identity a secret. They told us what the Portuguese colonial government did when they found an illegal Namibian in Angola. Firstly, they arrested the person, who was locked up in jail and in most cases subjected to hard labour. Then, they negotiated with the South African colonial government in Namibia about how and when to extradite the Namibian. Upon release from jail, the person was taken to Namibia under police escort and handed directly to the apartheid police. We were told clearly that because we did not possess the correct documents to travel through or live in Angola, we should avoid making ourselves targets for the Caetano army and police. Our situation was worsened by the fact that we were travelling through Angola to join SWAPO in Tanganyika. SWAPO was a liberation movement fighting against the apartheid colonial government in Namibia, which was an ally of the Portuguese colonial government in Angola. Therefore, we were always very secretive about our identity and origin as we did not want to compromise our safety.

During this period, there were two liberation movements fighting for the independence of Angola, the FNLA (*Frente Nacional de Libertação de Angola*) and the MPLA (*Movimiento Popular de Liberación de Angola*).[16] The relationship between these two movements was not hostile, but they did not really work together. We made sure not to take sides in the local Angolan politics, even though it had proven very difficult to remain neutral in this situation of extreme political conflict. If the Portuguese colonial officials in Angola found you amongst FNLA or MPLA supporters, they would consider you a supporter and therefore an enemy, no matter the circumstances. This was therefore a very difficult time to travel to Tanganyika through Angola.

Some of the Angolans with whom we survived at Nambuangongo told us stories about their sociopolitical survival strategies at the time, when the two liberation movements and the Portuguese colonial regime were competing for the support of the masses. Most of them

---

16 MPLA was the People's Movement for the Liberation of Angola. UNITA (União Nacional para a Independência Total de Angola, or in English, the National Union for the Total Independence of Angola) had not yet been formed at this time. FNLA (see footnote 14) was also colloquially referred to as OPA or UPA, and seemed very popular amongst the people.

supported both liberation movements. They also told us that there was a time when it was required of them to have membership cards for each movement. And, when soldiers from the liberation movements visited their homes, the family members would try to distinguish which movement the soldiers were from by examining their physical features, their Portuguese accent, their character and behaviour, the colour of their uniform, and what type of badges and medals they were wearing. If need be, they would then present the membership card of the relevant liberation movement. They also said that although the soldiers of the liberation movements did not go around asking the civilian population about their political loyalties, there had been times when political loyalty had saved their lives. Luckily, we did not face this problem during our travels in Angola, and the FNLA soldiers only ever assisted us in the spirit of solidarity and comradeship.

******

When the war in Nambuangongo subsided a little, we were provided with the opportunity to continue our journey. With the help of FNLA soldiers, we left Nambuangongo and continued through the Congo towards Tanganyika. There were about thirteen people in our group, and we faced the journey on foot. We walked slowly but surely northward towards the Congo until we arrived at a certain village where we were advised against going further northward. We spent about a week at this village because we were tired and needed to rest. We also needed to gather information about the area, the dangerous routes which had to be avoided, and the more advisable paths on which to travel.

Several people briefed us about the safe routes to the Congo border. It became clear that different people had had different experiences in the area. Some people dramatised the situation to the point where I did not even want to think about facing the journey. Others told us positive, wonderful stories of people who had journeyed successfully into the Congo. They encouraged us to go on. In order to plan our journey, we had to carefully weigh all this information. We later realised that routes that had been recommended as safe at one time suddenly became dangerous at another time. It all depended on how the Portuguese forces were controlling the border.

From this village, the name of which I can now not remember, we were strongly advised not to cross the Congo River from Angola directly into the Congo. This route was apparently deadly dangerous as the Portuguese army and police were very active on the border here. The safer route was to get into the Congo via Cabinda.[17] We were advised to walk in a northwest direction and cross the Congo River from Angola into Cabinda. There was a ferry that took people from the Angolan side of the river to Cabinda. As Cabinda was part of Angolan territory, no documents were required to travel there. All that was needed was payment for the ferry.

The Portuguese colonial troops were deployed along the Congo border to prevent Angolans from crossing into the Congo, and Congolese from crossing into Angola. Caetano soldiers were apparently under strict orders to shoot dead any person who approached the border before they had the chance to cross into the neighbouring territory. Our Angolan comrades informed us that the tight security along the border had begun with the coming to power of Patrice Lumumba as Prime Minister of the Republic of the Congo in 1960. His power was seen as a threat to the Portuguese colonial government in Angola, which accused him of supporting the liberation movements. Apparently, Lumumba allowed the FNLA to establish military training camps in southern Congo, from where FNLA-trained combatants returned to Angola to fight the Portuguese colonial government for the independence of Angola. The Portuguese colonial government feared that Angolans crossing into the Congo might become potential FNLA soldiers.

It was evident that FNLA soldiers were trying to cross the Congo River into Angola to fight for their independence from Portuguese colonial rule, while the colonial government deployed its troops to ambush them before they could set foot on Angolan territory. We were urged to be extra careful and to look out for the movement of Caetano as we approached the Congo River because innocent lives had been lost.

---

17 Cabinda (also spelt Kabinda) is an exclave territory of Angola which was bordered to the east by Congo-Leopoldville, to the north by Congo-Brazzaville and to the west by the Atlantic Ocean.

The water points were the favourite ambush zones for the Portuguese military. We therefore needed to know where we could get drinking water without putting our lives at risk. We were advised to be quiet and alert in order not to give away our presence to the enemy. We were told that we should be sure to see the enemy first, and then hide. We were also told, in no uncertain terms, that Caetano had no mercy; that it made no difference that we were a group of many civilians crossing the border. They would simply shoot at us, collect our bodies, and set them on fire. We were advised that it was less dangerous if we crossed the Congo River from Angola into Cabinda, because Cabinda was part of Angolan territory.

Had it not been for the Angolans who had accompanied us on this journey, it is difficult to imagine how we would have faced it. The Angolans knew their country well, they spoke the local languages, especially Portuguese, and they understood the culture and customs of the Angolan people. Having them with us was a real advantage to us. They understood and shared the spirit of standing up to fight against colonialism. These Angolans were not merely accompanying us. They too were going to join their liberation movement, FNLA, which was operating mainly along the Angola/Congo border.

We walked during the night to avoid being detected by Caetano spy planes. We slept or rested during the day in the shade of big trees, while two or three men went on short reconnaissance missions ahead. On their return, they would advise us regarding which route to take. They also brought us food.

On this part of the journey, Shikongo suddenly became overprotective of me. He started taking extra care of me to the extent that he did not want to leave my side. I was puzzled. I could not understand his sudden over-protectiveness. I then noticed that all the Namibian men had started to watch over me, and this really worried me. Later on they explained this behaviour to me. They said that they had noticed that our FNLA guides had been developing a questioning attitude towards me. It looked as though they may have been doubting my loyalty and were watching me more carefully to assess my commitment. This caused Shikongo and his compatriots to become worried sick.

They were concerned that the FNLA men may have planned to sacrifice me. So Shikongo literally became my bodyguard, and when he was not around, the other Namibian men took over. This situation could have arisen because I have a very light complexion. I cannot explain it. I was born with a very light skin. This was not a good situation.

Yet the Angolan comrades were very well-versed regarding the terrain of their country, and they guided us skilfully throughout this journey. Each day, as soon as the sun had begun to set and the sky had turned orange in the west, our guides advised us to move on. The distance from the village where we had first received our information to Cabinda was not very far, but the security threat posed by the Caetano military presence forced us to walk in circles sometimes to avoid the enemy. We had to walk stealthily, and we made very little daily progress.

It was an arduous and very dangerous journey. We were tense and anxious. At some point, the journey seemed never-ending and I totally gave up. I accepted that we would all die in the Angolan forest and we would never get to Tanganyika. We seemed to have run out of options. Death was the only answer, and the only question was when it would strike. I denied myself thoughts of home, and suppressed my memories of the family I had left behind. Even today, as I am relating this story to you, I feel cold shivers running down my spine because I did not think that I would survive that journey and be able to relate this experience, as I am doing now. I am grateful to the Angolan people who treated us like their own and shared with us whatever they had, under very difficult circumstances.

Then, suddenly, we arrived at the Congo River, and were waiting to cross by ferry into Cabinda. We were advised to look normal and not to carry any worries on our faces. We crossed the river on a big ferry. On arrival in Cabinda, I was shocked when the local people gave us mealie meal to eat. Later on they told us that when the war had started, the Portuguese people had frantically fled Cabinda to find shelter and security in Luanda. They had left behind most of their belongings. Their houses had been left intact and their fields unharvested. The people of Cabinda had moved in at the speed of the wind and removed what they could carry from their properties, especially food items, and had transported it very quickly into the forest. They came up with a plan to bury food under the ground, and dug deep, long underground trenches where they stored the food to prevent it from being seen and bombed. The people of Cabinda had seemed to possess many tactics and strategies to survive the war. They were well organised and had an excellent community spirit. They shared whatever they had with each other in the spirit of comradeship and solidarity. Food was collected from the trenches on a weekly basis to feed everyone. The idea that food could expire, which we have today, had no place in our minds during our journey. Our stomachs accepted whatever food we were given, and we never got sick from eating tired-looking food.

******

As was advised by the villagers in Angola, crossing into the Congo from Cabinda was much easier. We still had to be careful, but the danger was not as overwhelming as it would have been if we had crossed the Congo River from Angola directly into the Congo under the watchful eye of the Portuguese army and police. On the day we arrived on Congolese soil, we found a big gathering of Angolans at a village near the border. This village had a receiving centre where refugees arriving from Angola stayed temporarily. We spent the next three months at this receiving centre, nearly starving to death. This village, the name of which I am trying in vain to recall, was hunger-stricken. There had been no SWAPO representative to receive us. The Angolans with whom we had come disappeared from sight the moment we arrived in the Congo. They went to the FNLA camps. Us Namibians were left there all on our own. We spoke an understandable Portuguese, which we had learnt during our travels through Angola, but in the Congo people spoke Lingala and French, which was completely foreign to us. So, when the Angolans left us, we felt really lost.

There was a general famine in the Congo. The local people took care of us by providing us with brown packets of powdered milk. This was our only food item. It was very tough to survive on powdered milk alone as our stomachs were not used to it. We later discovered that food was available in the small village market, but we did not have the money to buy it, and we did not understand the language spoken by the people of the Congo.

One day, I saw a Congolese man selling firewood. I watched people giving him money and in return he gave them firewood. I watched this over and over, and the idea came to me that I too could collect firewood from the forest and sell it to get money for food. This I then did. I sold the firewood for three francs a bundle. With this money I was able to buy enough mealie meal for dinner for five adults. If I was not too tired, I would return to the forest to collect another bundle of firewood to either sell or exchange directly for food. Shikongo decided that we should all go to the forest to collect firewood and sell it. Soon we had enough money to buy food. The idea then came to us that we should continue to sell firewood until we had enough money to cover our bus fares from this village up to Leopoldville.[18] So, we collected firewood like crazy and sold all of it until we had enough money to continue our journey.

******

On arrival in Leopoldville, we asked around for directions to the offices of the liberation movements. Luckily, every now and then we found people who spoke Portuguese, which we had learnt in Angola. The Congolese people were very helpful. We told them we were Namibians looking for SWAPO. They did not seem to know much about SWAPO, so they took us to the offices of the FNLA in Leopoldville. The officials whom we found at the FNLA office were also very helpful and received us in the spirit of solidarity and comradeship. They gave us a place to live, where we stayed for two months. They also provided us with food for the duration of our stay. When we arrived in the Congo, we did not have any presentable clothes. We were still wearing the clothes we had survived in during the bombing of Nambuangongo. The FNLA officials perhaps took pity on us and gave us clothes, nice clothes. They really treated us with kindness.

One day, in 1964, we heard that the president of SWAPO, President Sam Nujoma, was visiting the Congo and was actually in Leopoldville.

---

18 Present-day Kinshasa.

We decided to go and search for him. We were in luck. We found him and jumped on him on the spot. Comrade Jacob Kuhangwa had accompanied the president on this mission to the Congo. We told him who we were and that we were looking for SWAPO. We said we wanted to go to Tanganyika, but were struggling to get there. We told him all our problems, worries, concerns and wishes. On that same day, the president left Leopoldville and returned to Tanganyika. A few weeks later, a SWAPO representative by the name of Comrade Andreas Shipanga arrived in Leopoldville. He was sent by President Sam Nujoma to represent us. Oh, our conditions improved a great deal; our representative started to look after us. He bought food for us, including tinned beef and fish – an extreme luxury. *Tate*[19] Andreas Shipanga told us that he wanted to get us out of the Congo as soon as possible, but he did not tell us why. He started preparing travel documents for us and, within a few days, we had passports and plane tickets from Leopoldville to Northern Rhodesia.[20]

******

We left the Congo by plane to Lusaka in Northern Rhodesia. On arrival at the airport in Lusaka, a SWAPO representative by the name of Comrade Hifikepunye Lucas Pohamba[21] welcomed us warmly. He took us from the airport to a SWAPO house in Lusaka where we stayed for one week. After a week's rest, we continued our journey to Tanganyika. We were now in the hands of SWAPO, which made our journey very smooth. From Lusaka, we travelled alone by plane to Lilongwe in Nyasaland.[22] The people at the SWAPO office in Lusaka had given us very clear information on how to cover the rest of the journey on our own. We were told that on arrival in Nyasaland we should go from the

---

19 Oshiwambo form of address for an older man. It expresses both respect and endearment, and can be translated as 'father'.
20 Present-day Zambia. The name changed to Zambia after independence in October 1964 (later in that year).
21 Later, in independent Namibia, he became Secretary-General of SWAPO from 1997 to 2002 and Vice- President of SWAPO from 2002 to 2007. After holding various ministerial portfolios, he became Namibia's second President in 2005.
22 Present-day Malawi. The name changed to Malawi after independence in July 1964 (later in that year).

airport to the nearest bus station and buy tickets to the Mbeya Region in Tanganyika. On arrival in Nyasaland, we got onto a bus to Mbeya without wasting any time.

SOLDIER

3
MILITARY TRAINING IN KONGWA

I cannot remember the exact date, but it was during the month of July 1964 that we finally arrived in Tanganyika[23] after an eventful journey of more than a year, which had taken us from Namibia through Angola, the Congo, Northern Rhodesia and Nyasaland. I have also forgotten the name of the small town in the Mbeya Region which was our port of entry into Tanganyika. Two SWAPO representatives were there to meet us, namely Comrades Peter Katjavivi and Eliander Mwatale. They received us well, bought us food, and put us onto another bus that took us from the Mbeya Region to Dar es Salaam.

We arrived in Dar es Salaam in the early morning hours and found Comrades Peter Nanyemba and Peter Mweshihange waiting for our arrival. They welcomed us warmly and took us to a SWAPO house in Dar es Salaam. On arrival in Tanganyika, we immediately realised that we had indeed found our fellow countrymen who had left Namibia before us. They were well organised and had lobbied for support and recognition.

While I was in Dar es Salaam, Comrade Vinia Ndadi invited me to speak on the External Service of Radio Tanganyika.[24] The Tanganyika Broadcasting Corporation[25] had generously provided a radio slot for SWAPO to broadcast its plans and programmes to the whole world. This service was pioneered by Comrade Mosé Tjitendero, after which he was awarded a scholarship to study in the USA. He was succeeded by Comrade Nangolo Ithete, who soon afterwards also received a

---

23 The mainland of Tanzania became a German colony called Tanganyika in 1884 whilst the Sultanate of Zanzibar became a British Protectorate in 1890. Tanganyika became a British mandated territory in 1918 and achieved independence in 1961. In 1963 Zanzibar achieved independence, and a year later formed a union with Tanganyika called the United Republic of Tanganyika and Zanzibar, which later the same year was renamed Tanzania.
24 The name was later changed to Radio Tanzania.
25 The name was later changed to the Tanzania Broadcasting Corporation.

scholarship to study in Yugoslavia. Comrade Nicky Iyambo took over from Comrade Ithete, and not long after that he, too, was awarded a scholarship to study in Finland. SWAPO was actively looking for scholarships from all over the world to send its young people to study because education was at the centre of all its programmes and activities. Comrade Vinia Ndadi, who had recently arrived in Dar es Salaam from Namibia, was asked to take over from Comrade Iyambo. When we arrived, Comrade Ndadi was the Supervisor of SWAPO Programmes at the External Service of Radio Tanganyika. He invited me to talk on the radio about our journey, and to send a message of my choice to fellow Namibians and the world at large.

Radio was one of the most effective mediums for SWAPO to reach out to the world, and it was maximised and used effectively throughout the struggle. The programme 'Voice of Namibia' later expanded its broadcasting to Addis Ababa, Cairo, Lusaka, Luanda and Brazzaville. I was very happy for this opportunity to speak on the radio, especially because one could speak in the language of one's choice. I was illiterate and could not speak English, so I spoke in my mother tongue, Oshiwambo. I decided to tell my fellow Namibian listeners that Mukwanangobe Aguste yaImmanuel was greeting them from SWAPO, which was broadcasting from the External Service of Radio Tanganyika in Dar es Salaam. I said that Tanganyika was an independent African country that had liberated itself from colonial rule. The people of Tanganyika had fought for their independence, had won, and were now free from foreign domination. I informed them that Tanganyika was hosting us so that we could prepare to fight for our independence and be free, like most nations of the world.

I called on all able Namibians to join us in exile to receive the education which we were denied at home by the colonial government. I emphasised the importance of education to prepare ourselves for successfully administering our country after independence. I also called on all able Namibians to join our independence struggle and to stand together to rid our motherland of the enemy so that we could become independent like Tanganyika, from which the broadcast was coming. I said that we had to free ourselves from the yoke of colonialism and apartheid, and that if we just sat down and did nothing about the political situation in our country, no one would bring us independence on a silver platter.

I was very happy that my message had been heard by people in Namibia. I recall that when I met Comrade Nahas Angula[26] for the first time, he told me that he had heard me speaking on Voice of Namibia.

I think that the rest of our stay in Dar es Salaam was meant to give us an opportunity to recover from our arduous journey from Namibia. We stayed in the SWAPO house for about three months, and here I assumed the role of *Nampaafita* (giver to cattle herders)[27]. I also became a cook, which I was happy to do because in my culture I had been raised to fulfill this role. I was a great cook, too. During our stay in Dar es Salaam there was discussion about sending me to school, but I think these plans were shelved when SWAPO realised that I was illiterate, and maybe there were no adult literacy options. The SWAPO President, Comrade Sam Nujoma, requested that we go and live in his house in Dar es Salaam, at a place called Magomeni. This was where we stayed until we were told one day to pack our belongings and move on to Mbeya. We went there on the same bus that had initially brought us from Mbeya to Dar es Salaam.

In Mbeya, *Tate* Homateni Kalwenya and many other comrades welcomed us. We were accommodated together with our comrades in one big house in Morogoro. There were about twelve of us living in the same house. Life in Morogoro was a bit tough for me because I was the only woman amongst men. We were given living allowances from the UN. Our leaders collected the money from the UN office on our behalf, and bought food and other necessities for everyone.

* * * * * *

In 1965, the SWAPO leadership informed us that the Tanzanian[28] government had allocated us a place suitable for military training, called Kongwa. SWAPO therefore called upon all its members to go to Kongwa to receive military and combat training, or to train others. Kongwa

---

26 Later, in independent Namibia, Comrade Angula held several ministerial portfolios and rose to the position of Prime Minister from 2006 to 2012.
27 A girl born amongst a family of boys is often called *Nampaafita* meaning 'giver to cattle-herders'. Boys are associated with cattle herding and the name comes from this background.
28 In 1963, Zanzibar achieved independence, and in 1964 formed a union with Tanganyika called the United Republic of Tanganyika and Zanzibar, which was renamed Tanzania later in the same year.

became the first SWAPO military training camp outside Namibia. So, like many of my comrades, I left for Kongwa.

When we arrived at Kongwa, I was still a village girl, very nice and soft. I was constantly intimidated by the men, and was still trying to play the girl role from my childhood upbringing. The man's world I was now entering was foreign to me. An adjustment was needed, but there was no mentor for me, only the reality of the situation in which I found myself, which was to undergo military training. I was feminine, very nervous, and did not know how to talk back or chat to my male comrades. What was I to discuss with them, how was I to fit into their conversations? I did not know anything about cattle posts, hunting or the contract labour system. They spoke about places such as Cape Town, Cairo, Egypt, Abyssinia and many others. I became totally lost because, apart from reading about Egypt in the Bible, I had never been to any of these places. I could not take part in the discussions and felt out of place. Some of the comrades used to tease me or tell me stories about places I had never heard of before. I was uncomfortable about this, and sometimes I accepted what they told me as the truth even when it was meant to be a joke.

As a child, I was socialised to behave in a polite and respectful manner toward others in our community, especially towards adults and particularly towards men. Everything I did or said was in the spirit of my Christian faith, which was deeply entrenched. I carried these values with me to Kongwa, where my comrades started to make jokes about me and tease me so badly that I sometimes went to my room and cried. I started going to the Evangelical Lutheran Church service in Morogoro every single Sunday without fail, and returned to Kongwa afterwards. The service was carried out in the Swahili language, which I did not understand. But I went nonetheless because I felt spiritually uplifted being in church, and also being amongst a group of people – women, children and men. This was something I did not have in the camp, where I was the only woman. Going to church was very therapeutic for me. I eventually learned Swahili and speak it fluently to this day.

During my first weeks at Kongwa, I found the company of men very intimidating. They always spoke about politics – every day, every hour – unless we were in the training sessions. The moment the training session ended, their political discussions began, and would go on and on. Their brains were infused with political ideology, and they thought of nothing else but politics. Whenever they were together eating, it was always politics. They spoke about politics throughout breakfast, lunch and dinner. During leisure time we received news, which was followed by heated political debates. I did not know anything about politics, so I had nothing to say. I became angry with these men. They would talk about their politics around me whether I wanted to listen or not.

As if the intimidating political discussions were not enough, the men decided unilaterally to change my name from Mukwanangobe (my paternal totem) to Mukwahepo (*mukwa* referring to 'belonging' and *hepo* which comes from the word *oluhepo* which means 'poverty', so 'one who belongs to the poor clan').[29] They called me Mukwahepo, to tease me because of my situation – a woman alone in a military training camp; a woman amongst men in the liberation struggle movement (in other words, 'the poor thing'). Mukwahepo became my name and has remained so ever since, no matter how hard I tried to tell my comrades that I was Mukwanangobe. It was like talking to deaf ears. Aguste yaImmanuel was never heard of again, except on formal papers.

******

All the trainees at Kongwa gave themselves new names, combat names. As the training intensified, I became politically indoctrinated and I also thought that this was a great opportunity to abandon Mukwahepo. I therefore proudly announced my combat name to all my comrades. I told them that my name was Namumbaduka:

Aame Namumbaduka	My name is Namumbaduka
Onyofi yokeengula	the morning star
Yambadukila moKongwa	shining upon Kongwa
Moshilongo shaNyerere	in the land of Nyerere[30]

---

29 See footnote 3.
30 A reference to Julius Nyerere, the first Prime Minister and President of Tanganyika (renamed Tanzania in 1964).

Namumbaduka is an Oshiwambo name that is common in our culture and refers to the morning star (*mawila*), which is an important landmark and icon for many young people; a guide for many of the traditional tasks they are expected to perform. It is the star that never fails to wake up. Namumbaduka rises when it should and provides light and direction to the universe. As it always rises in the east and journeys to the west, it is a very dependable landmark that never fails anyone. It is like a traditional alarm clock, waking all the girls in the community to go and pound mahangu. When someone wanted to go somewhere very early in the morning – even today when most people own watches – they would say, 'I will leave early in the morning, as soon as the morning star begins to rise in the east.' Even when we were in the camps, many of us did not have watches. But we relied on the morning star to get out of bed before the enemy could come and find us sleeping. So the name Namumbaduka is very iconic, and it inspired me to emulate its motherly nature – the giver of light and direction to humanity.

We developed a culture of using combat names, the idea behind which was to simply provide security or cover for ourselves by keeping our true identities unknown. Even our comrades did not know our real names, or from what village we originated in Namibia. This was important because if one of us was captured by the enemy, it was more difficult for that person to disclose information about other comrades in the camp. Only knowing one another by our combat names therefore provided more security for everyone. Furthermore, these were not only combat names but also praise names. We named ourselves after something or someone we respected, looked up to, or considered courageous, charismatic or inspiring. We needed to be inspired into courage to fight for and win our independence.

Although I gave myself the name Namumbaduka, it was never used. No one called me by it. My comrades had decided to call me Mukwahepo and nothing more. They were stuck to Mukwahepo, no matter what. I slowly realised that however hard I tried to avoid the name Mukwahepo, no one would call me Namumbaduka or Aguste. So, I made peace with my name. I was slowly getting used to my comrades at Kongwa as individuals and found myself talking back to them in the same manner as they addressed me, and as freely as I saw fit. All of a sudden, they stopped teasing me. Mukwahepo, however, was the only thing they did not give up. So I became Mukwahepo, then and forever after.

After nearly three months of feeling out of place, I started accepting my situation and decided to make the best of every opportunity. Suddenly, strange things began to happen within me, and they happened very fast. It seemed that as I was listening to the men talking, I was picking up the issues and, one day, I simply found myself at the centre of political talks. I was now becoming politically aware and was challenging the men.

******

Every month that we were at Kongwa, the camp authorities gave each of us a jar of Vaseline and a bar of soap. I did not know where these things were coming from, but I assumed that it was part of the support we were being given by the Tanzanian government. Considering that the personal items distributed to us at Kongwa were bought from the local Tanzanian shops, I expected that they would include some special provisions for me. This never happened – I was given the same supplies as my male comrades, and when my moon came, I merely struggled to manage my cycle as best I could and carry on with my training duties. Seemingly, the people who were shopping for the Kongwa trainees did not know that there was a woman amongst us. It seemed that men bought the clothing for the men at Kongwa. This never bothered me as I became used to wearing men's underwear and clothing. When I was in desperate need, I went to Dr Peter Shinyafa Haitembu, the camp doctor, who – depending on the availability – sometimes gave me a bundle of cotton wool to use as sanitary pads.

Shyness at exposing my monthly female condition was my biggest challenge. I still cannot understand why I felt too shy to tell anyone that I was having my period, which is a natural condition for all women. Yet during our training this was my biggest secret. I made sure that my comrades did not find out my moon cycle. I felt I could not just announce to my trainer that I was unable to attend classes due to period cramps. It was easier to say that I had a headache. Shyness was my biggest enemy, and until I overcame this, I had problems expressing myself.

Our training was tough, and during my periods I could not make it without sanitary pads. So I had to face Dr Haitembu every time my cycle came, to ask him to provide me with cotton wool. He was not always so generous with the cotton wool. He seemed to ration it strictly. I remember one day when I needed it very badly and he only gave me a very small piece. Perhaps this was because, not being a woman, he had no understanding of what menstruation involved. I took the cotton wool, knowing it would not be enough. Later, I sent Shikongo to talk to him, and from then on things changed.

One day, I was surprised to see that face powder was amongst the items that were sent to Kongwa. This was given to me. However, throughout my stay I never received sanitary pads or women's underwear. My travels from Angola to Tanzania had taught me many things and had prepared me to face many situations. I later realised that, as the first woman in the SWAPO camps, I was meant to go through this experience in order to prepare a better training environment for my fellow women comrades who came to Kongwa after me. It was very important for them to provide women in training with the essential amenities because this would greatly enhance their full participation in the training activities. I had proven the point that, like our male comrades, women could face both military training and combat. I never fought a single battle, but I was well trained and combat-ready.

******

While I was at Kongwa, I heard that a Namibian woman by the name of Comrade Libertina Apollus had arrived in Dar es Salaam. I was overjoyed to receive this news and started planning how we would share the space of my room at Kongwa. I eagerly awaited her arrival but, once I realised that this was not going to happen, I asked permission of our camp commander to go to Dar es Salaam to meet her. You have no idea what it meant to me to have a fellow Namibian woman joining the struggle in exile. I longed to meet my sister, Comrade Apollus, whom I felt I had known for hundreds of years. I wanted a sister to talk to and relate to. After making inquiries, our camp commander informed me that she was a highly educated woman and that SWAPO had already sent her to school to further her studies in medicine. I therefore did not get the opportunity to meet her at that point. I was happy for her, yet at the same time I was sad because I really looked forward to having some women comrades with me in the camp. When she returned from school, I was still at Kongwa. Then, one day we received the great news that she and Comrade Ben Amathila had married in Dar es Salaam. I left Tanzania without having had the opportunity to meet my sister face to face, but deep in my heart I held her very dear. My opportunity to meet her arrived later, in Zambia.

******

At Kongwa we received political education, as well as guerrilla warfare training and combat training. Our instructors were the late Comrade Agustus Nghaamwa, popularly known by his combat name, McNamara, and Comrade Julius Shilongo, whose combat name was Kashuku. Commander McNamara taught us that guerrilla warfare was based on the fact that the enemy against whom we were fighting was very powerful, with many soldiers, and with weapons that were more sophisticated than ours. In order to be successful when we engaged with the enemy on the battlefield, we had to come up with military tactics of which they were unaware.

We adopted a guerrilla military strategy whereby our combat soldiers, instead of engaging the enemy in open battle, would attack when the enemy was unaware of our presence. The idea was to attack at strategic points, in secret. If we engaged our enemy in open battle, we would be defeated because the enemy had the transport capacity to bring in reinforcements quickly, on land as well as in the air. Guerrilla warfare would allow us to establish small but powerful units that would attack very fast and then retreat before the enemy had a chance to respond. The small guerrilla units were also intended to create panic in the enemy camp. Our main aim was to fight the enemy in secrecy so that we could win the war both physically and psychologically. We also used guerrilla maneouvers to confuse the enemy and to cover our tracks so that it was difficult for them to follow our footprints, or find out where we had come from or retreated to.

During guerrilla warfare training, we were taught about survival strategies under battlefront conditions that ranged from normal to very extreme. This training included learning how to 'take cover', a military term meaning to lie completely flat on the ground and assume a shooting position. Guerrilla soldiers cannot fight a battle in a standing position, except for those who are operating mortars and long-range or artillery weapons. We learnt how to take cover and to move quickly from one place to another by rolling along the ground, or by crawling. These were important skills which allowed us to escape without being seen by the enemy. The other survival method was to wear camouflage uniforms to try to conceal ourselves and blend in with the natural surroundings so as not to be an obvious target. For instance, a combatant wearing a green and brown uniform is less noticeable when in a tree guarding over others because the colour of the clothing and the tree are similar.

We also learnt the symbols of our organisation. We had to know by heart all the markers of our corporate identity, such as our logo, uniform, badges, shoes, hats and weapons, as well as the behaviour of our group. We learnt to observe and memorise all military signs and behaviour, for instance, we had to identify our footprints and distinguish them from those of the enemy. We also learnt to distinguish military footprints from civilian ones. Walking in single file was another tactic we learnt, and we were able to roughly tell how many people had walked through a place in single file. All the many things we learnt during this training were important, useful life skills for combat soldiers. All of them could make a difference in saving one's life.

Guerrilla fighters are trained to always be level-headed, clear and focused. If you come across the enemy by surprise, you do not just open fire on them. You must first study the enemy and observe how many of them there are and what type of weapons they have. You must measure the strength of the enemy against the strength of your group. A guerrilla fighter must also establish whether the enemy is alone or is part of a larger contingent, and whether the enemy soldiers are following your tracks or are merely on patrol. You only attack them if this is the most viable option, first ensuring that if you were to retreat, you would not be retreating into an enemy ambush.

As we were being trained to face the enemy in combat, our practical sessions were all based on real-life situations that we may have come across on the battlefield. During our training, we did a lot of marching and climbing mountains, as well as running – serious running – as you would do if a lion was chasing you. Commander Kashuku taught us how to march like combat soldiers. He drilled us over and over until we were physically fit. Using the Arabic drill commanding system (*star-hop, star-raa, star-hop, meem-cee, hop-hei, hop-hei, academ slaa-hack*), he trained us every day until he was satisfied that we were fit enough to face even more difficult training.

At the beginning, I was embarrassed to take part in physical training because I was uneasy about lifting my legs high up, as was required by the drilling exercises. I was a modest woman and this was asking too much. According to my upbringing, women are meant to keep their legs together, yet I found myself being required to lift up my legs to the level of my hips. The first week was therefore a total flop, and as I was training, all kinds of questions went through my mind. I wondered why I was in Tanzania and why I had joined the struggle. After pondering these questions, I decided that if this was what it took to gain our freedom and independence, like the people of Tanzania had done, then fine, I would do it. So, I got over it and decided to just get on with it.

On my first day of training, I was sweating like a pig. It was tough exercise and I had no way of escaping it. I therefore made peace with it. I tried to be brave and have fun with it. On the second day, my entire body was sore. My legs, arms and stomach muscles ached to the bone. Despite this, Commander Kashuku continued to call out orders – *star-hop, star-raa, hop-hei, hop-hei*. Fortunately, the human body adjusts quickly, and soon the pain disappeared and we became physically fit. We climbed and jumped from high objects. This training was serious business, and our political education helped us to understand why it was necessary. Obedience and discipline is an important aspect of any military training. An undisciplined army would be no army at all because the soldiers would just do as they liked and there would be chaos. An army requires a clear line of authority. The soldiers have to respect authority. Yet although we took our training seriously, it was also fun.

We had several guns in the camp and learnt the names of them all, one by one. Our commanders taught us how to operate each one of them. We were trained to use different types of weapons, such as semi-automatics, carbines, pepesa, bazookas, mortars, and many others. We were also trained to use hand grenades and to recognise and explode landmines. We learnt how to dismantle guns, how to clean and oil them properly, and how to reassemble them. Our commanders also taught us how to load the magazines and keep them at safety. This had to be done very quickly, and we were timed. We were expected to do it faster each time. Eventually, some of us were quicker than our instructors. The guns were greasy, and we had to assemble them on the ground without allowing any sand to get into them.

We also learnt how to repair a gun. During the training, we had to imagine a scenario whereby we were in a battle and our gun failed to fire. The enemy fire was coming thick and fast, and it had to be repelled. We therefore had to repair our gun speedily and return to battle. There could be several reasons why a gun failed to fire. It could be due to rust or dirt, or because the parts were not assembled correctly. Having a thorough knowledge of each of the guns we used was essential to our understanding of which of them gave us the competitive advantage over the enemy's weapons. To fight successfully, it is important to know the military strength of one's enemy.

Commander Kashuku gave us shooting lessons and taught us how to aim at a target. He was fast but kind, and had the patience to explain until everyone understood. In between all of this, we had to drill, drill and drill. He also gave us running and exercise lessons. On top of this, we were given a political education which, among other things, involved developing the characteristics of good guerrilla fighters. We had to learn what behaviour and character traits our fellow comrades and the civilian population expected of a SWAPO freedom fighter. SWAPO freedom fighters were expected to be alert at all times of the day and night, in wartime or when they were at leisure. Commander Kashuku taught us the tactics required to face very tough situations, such as being captured in combat, and how to avoid disclosing information that would be critical for the survival of one's fellow comrades. Anyone who has been in a war will tell you that it is no holiday to be captured by the enemy because you are forced to reveal the whereabouts of your comrades. A good freedom fighter must never bring the enemy into the comrade's camp, and must never reveal the whereabouts of the other comrades. Every combatant has the responsibility to protect the safety and security of all the comrades, as well as military logistics. When freedom fighters fall into enemy hands, they are expected to sacrifice themselves for the safety and security of the others, always bearing in mind the ultimate goal – the total liberation of the motherland.

SWAPO freedom fighters were not supposed to allow themselves to become chatterboxes. They were expected to refrain from talking too much, especially in public places. A talkative person often runs out of words, and in the end begins to talk about military logistics. This situation may end up compromising the success of a plan or mission, as well as the security of others. Garrulousness was discouraged throughout our training because we had political commissars who were specifically trained for mass mobilisation, which required verbal communication skills. Talkative people often ended up regretting things they had said, realising the serious consequences of their words only after they had been said, by which time it was too late.

******

We left the Kongwa military training camp with the clear understanding that if a fully armed freedom fighter was amongst the civilian population, that person should remain calm and collected at all times and should refrain from moving around in an agitated fashion. Unpredictable behaviour by a freedom fighter is extremely dangerous because it may scare civilians, the very people that freedom fighter is supposed to protect. Such behaviour might also cause civilians to be frightened of the organisation that the freedom fighter represents. The weapons carried by a freedom fighter are supposed to provide security and protection to the public, but if they are abused when brought into the broader social environment, this might become a danger to public safety. Every freedom fighter who was trained at Kongwa knew what behaviour they were expected to adopt, especially when mingling with the civilian population.

The other thing we were taught was to control our behaviour regarding alcohol. Freedom fighters should stay away from alcohol and from drinking establishments. They should not go around drinking alcohol like fish swallowing water in the sea and end up totally drunk and useless. A drunk combatant, whose behaviour is unpredictable and difficult to control, is disastrous, catastrophic and a total embarrassment to the organisation and to the spirit of freedom and liberation. That person may do or say something which could cause damage to the organisation. Alcohol and drunkenness bring about disgrace, and compromise the spirit of solidarity and commitment to the independence struggle. Drunkenness was therefore not condoned or tolerated. It was understood that a true freedom fighter would never get drunk, but would choose to abstain from alcohol because the fight for freedom was far more important than the personal pleasure (if any) that one may experience from alcohol consumption.

******

Our instructors informed us that they were training us with the ultimate aim of returning to Namibia to fight against the South African apartheid government that had colonised our country. We had to be properly trained in order to fight well so that we could defeat our colonisers and achieve freedom and independence for Namibia. Once independent, we would establish our government based on the ideology of socialism, whereby every citizen would enjoy the fruits of independence. We were told about the solidarity and comradeship inherent in socialist political thinking. Socialists were supposed to wish for one another all the good things they wished for themselves. According to socialist thinking, the problems of one's fellow citizens are experienced and considered as though they are one's own.

Another important component of our training concerned the things we learnt through talking to one another and through the often heated discussions and debates we had amongst ourselves. This discussion was usually triggered by the news we heard on the radio. We listened to radio news every single day without fail, the only exception being when our radio batteries were flat and when we did not have enough money to buy new ones. We listened to international radio news and news from our own SWAPO radio stations, which first started broadcasting from Radio Tanzania in Dar es Salaam and Cairo, and later expanded to Lusaka, Luanda and Brazzaville.[31] Radio was an excellent platform for SWAPO to articulate its vision and mandate in a mature and responsible manner, and to neutralise any false information which was being disseminated by enemy broadcasts. Information was both an important resource and a powerful tool during our struggle.

We also listened to the enemy radio news programmes, broadcast by the SABC and the SWABC.[32] There were times when the enemy radio stations used negative propaganda against our organisation. They called SWAPO a 'terrorist organisation' and accused us of being 'communists who do not believe in God'. Other radio stations (our friends and supporters) referred to us as 'freedom fighters' or 'defenders of justice and of the peoples' rights and freedoms'.

It was important to listen to our enemy's propaganda in order to understand their thinking and to develop counter strategies. Our comrades who worked for the SWAPO radio station smartly countered the enemy propaganda. Furthermore, we really enjoyed listening to the radio and appreciated the broadcasts we heard from our SWAPO comrades. Radio news comprised a huge component of our political education, and we learnt without realising it. The Namibian independence struggle, as well as the struggles of other oppressed peoples in the world, was very topical in the news worldwide. The mutual support and encouragement amongst oppressed peoples was also very strong. This was a time when the motto, 'An injury to one is an injury to all' meant something because many people were in solidarity with one another.

By listening to the radio news, we were able to distinguish which organisations and governments were our friends and supporters, and which were our enemies. When people were interviewed on the radio or asked to make statements about the situation in Namibia or South

---

31 These broadcasts were called 'Voice of Namibia' and 'Namibia Hour'.
32 SABC – South African Broadcasting Corporation; SWABC – South West African Broadcasting Corporation.

Africa, you could tell their affiliation both from the content of their words and from the language they used. If people referred to SWAPO as a 'terrorist organisation', it was clear to us that they were our enemy, or they supported our enemy. We did not need to be told outright. Believe me, we had many enemies, especially amongst the richest nations of the world. We knew immediately that people were our friends and supporters when they used words like 'liberation movement' or 'freedom fighter'.

While a major part of our political consciousness was a result of listening to radio news, this consciousness was enhanced by the discussions and debates that went on amongst ourselves after the news every day. These were not merely reactions to or reflections on what we had heard. We were also developing tactics with which to win the support of those governments and organisations that were in a strategic position to support our struggle. Our goal was to fight and defeat our enemy, and to do this we needed to fully understand how our opponents were reacting to the political and military events of the day, and how they were thinking. Our discussions also focused on those organisations and countries that supported our enemy. We had to ask ourselves what they actually knew about us, apart from the propaganda they were given by our enemy.

I never had the opportunity of acquiring a formal education at school. I was illiterate when I left Namibia, and remained illiterate throughout the struggle. By illiterate I mean that I could read and write in my mother tongue, and nothing more. Despite the possibility of going to school in Tanzania in the 1960s, I did not have the basic educational foundations and was too old to go to primary school amongst small children. So the opportunity was lost. Furthermore, I did not feel strongly that I was missing anything by not going to school. I was content being at Kongwa, where I felt I had an important role to play. If you talk to people who were with me at Kongwa, they will tell you that there were instances when even the camp commander could not resolve an issue. Then Mukwahepo had to be called in to sort out the matter.

My presence at Kongwa was valued, and I felt I was making a difference. I was fulfilling a very important role, especially at the beginning of our struggle. Therefore, Kongwa was for me more than just a military training camp. It was the place where I learnt very important life skills, such as how to calm my anger, how to give others the opportunity to speak, and how to listen carefully without being judgmental. These skills helped me a great deal later on when I worked with children.

******

Things did not work out well between Shikongo and I while we were at Kongwa. Many issues came between us, and in the end we decided that it would be best for both of us to break up our intimate relationship. Our friendship improved after our separation; in fact, Shikongo became a great friend. Fortunately, our separation did not cause bitterness between us but strengthened our brotherly and sisterly love for each other. Shikongo had always treated me like a younger sister and was often over-protective of me. Although that was sometimes a bit much, I enjoyed his attention. It was nice to have someone playing the role of protector and big brother.

While we were at Kongwa, Shikongo was the first (and often the only) person I consulted when I was confronted with a problem, no matter how small or big. He would advise me as to how to tackle or solve the problem. My male comrades at Kongwa frequently went into the town of Morogoro for all kinds of things. Whenever Shikongo went with them and found things that were useful for women, such as scented soap or sanitary pads, he always bought them for me if he had enough money. He was one of very few men at Kongwa who understood that women have special needs and may react differently to men under certain circumstances, including physical or military training. He was my best friend and I could talk to him as if he was my older brother.

I was the first and only woman amongst men at Kongwa. It was hard for me, especially at the beginning, to adapt to this new life. It was difficult to find the space for myself to do my private things, as a woman.

For example, when I was having my periods during combat training, there were times when I needed to wash and change my sanitary pad after the morning session and before going for lunch. This was important in order for me to feel comfortable with myself and everyone around me. It was difficult to explain to the instructor that I needed to be excused for this, especially as discussing my private matters with my male comrades did not always go down well. They were ever-ready to tease the hell out of me. Shikongo had become my mind reader, and was always the first person to come to my aid. He conscientised the men – and especially the leadership – at Kongwa until they understood that although I was a trainee like everybody else, I was also a woman and had special needs. My problems and issues were difficult to announce publicly at the parade, for everyone to know. Shikongo's intervention helped our instructors to become more gender-sensitive. Eventually, when I asked to be excused from a training session, they stopped playing tough with me. They accepted my excuses without questioning me or requiring further details.

I have a lot of respect for Shikongo shaHangala, and appreciate how he led me through many difficulties and dangerous situations on our journey into exile. We went through a lot together, and this has remained a treasure in my heart. Despite the dangerous paths we travelled, he never gave up hope. He firmly believed that we would get to Tanganyika, and we did. We could have lost our way in Angola, but Shikongo was always positive. He knew me well and understood me better than anyone at Kongwa. I will never forget him. My life story cannot be told without him. It would be incomplete without the role he played in it.

******

Although we were given military training, we were clearly told that the question of Namibian independence was in the hands of the UN, the organisation which was preparing to free us. We were urged to respect and follow the UN's decisions. We were told that the UN would order

South Africa out of our country, and we knew that Ethiopia and Liberia were working actively around the clock to engage the UN and the international community to this end. Although we were being prepared for war, we understood that this war would only take place in the event of the failure of the UN's plans for Namibia.

We had been convinced that the solution to our struggle would come from the UN, and we believed this. Then, in 1966, a complaint against South Africa's continued presence in Namibia was brought to the International Court of Justice (ICJ) in The Hague by Ethiopia and Liberia. The ICJ dismissed the complaint. This unwelcome news was a big shock to us, more so because we had discussed this issue over and over during our conversations and debates. There were always some comrades who urged us to think about what would happen if the UN plan for a solution to the Namibian problem did not work out. These comrades had repeatedly asked what we were going to do if the UN abandoned our case. They had said that we could not put all our eggs in the UN basket.

I also think that the SWAPO leaders had been monitoring how the question of Namibia was being handled by the international community. I am sure that Kongwa had been established due to the strategic assessment that if Plan A had not worked out, in other words, if the UN did not help us, Plan B would be in place. We had to be ready to help ourselves. The decision of the ICJ showed us that the international community had turned their backs on us. We felt that they had no confidence in our ability to govern ourselves. We also felt that they were unconcerned about our suffering under the brutal apartheid regime. We felt urged to engage our colonisers in a military confrontation as it had now become evident that UN-mediated solutions would not yield results. It had become clear to us that if we did not fight for our independence, no one else would. So the ICJ decision was a turning point in our struggle. Our military training activities were vigorously intensified in anticipation of a shift from diplomatic efforts to the active pursuit of independence through both diplomacy and military engagement.[33]

******

Kongwa was the only place in southern Africa where SWAPO trained its combatants during the 1960s and early 1970s. However, some SWAPO comrades were sent for military training to countries as far afield as Egypt, Algeria, Ghana, China and the Soviet Union. Upon completion of their military training, these combatants returned to Kongwa, where they were redeployed and reassigned new responsibilities. In 1965, a year before the ICJ decision, plans were made to send six such comrades back to Namibia. Their mission was to prepare the Namibian people for the possible liberation struggle, just in case the UN plans did not work out. I cannot remember the names of all of these men, but I do know that Comrade Patrick Israel Iyambo (Lungada) was amongst them. When these comrades came to Kongwa and were being prepared for their mission to Namibia, we did not get to know them at all. We saw them only briefly at the parade and, before we knew it, they were heading to Namibia. I think the reason I remember that Comrade Israel Iyambo was amongst them is because he was the youngest, or perhaps because of the biblical connection with his name, Israel. The six comrades left Tanzania by car for Zambia, from where they went on foot to Namibia. In the meantime, we continued with our training at Kongwa.

The six comrades left. Days turned into weeks and weeks into months, and we did not hear anything about whether they had arrived in Namibia or how they were getting along with their mission. It was well over a year when we heard that, on 26 August 1966, they had

---

33 The case brought by Ethiopia and Liberia to the ICJ was rejected on the grounds that the applicant countries had no standing in the matter and that the UN was in fact the competent legal body to bring the case. It was acknowledged that there had been human rights violations in South West Africa (as it was then called). The South African government presented this ICJ 'judgement' as a major legal and political victory over Ethiopia and Liberia, and the court ruling in favour of South Africa dashed the hopes and expectations of the Namibian people for a peaceful deliverance from South African occupation. This judgement marked the turning point in the strategy for the struggle for an independent Namibia. In 1971 the ICJ gave an "advisory opinion" which ruled that South Africa was illegally occupying Namibia.

engaged the enemy in a battle at Omugulugwoombashe in the forest of Uukwaluudhi in northern Namibia. This date became a landmark in our struggle for liberation because it was the first time SWAPO freedom fighters had engaged the enemy in a battle inside Namibia. We also heard that after this battle the comrades were captured by the enemy, one by one, and that Comrade Lungada was the only one who had survived.

We did not want to listen to this bad news. This mission had been well planned, and SWAPO had sent its prime combatants. These men were selected because of their outstanding character traits. How could the enemy swallow them? We had more questions than we had answers.

In war, there are certain things one learns without being told. When our people had engaged with the enemy in battle, the information about the fallen, the wounded and the missing in action was not made known. However, if that person was married, his wife was usually officially informed. This was the case even with the battle at Omugulugwoombashe. We only came to hear about it much later. After that, the 26th of August became an important day in the SWAPO calendar. It became a day to remember the bravery and heroism of our heroes, a day of honour and glory and self-sacrifice. We commemorate our comrades' dedication to the struggle for Namibian independence.

After Omugulugwoombashe, the launching of military offensives through Zambia and Angola was considered the best option. We hoped that Angola would gain independence soon, and that its new government would allow us greater access and passage into Namibia to fight for our own independence.[34] We wanted to maintain friendly relations with the people of Angola because we needed their solidarity and support.

Our leaders took a decision to send some comrades to Namibia through Angola. These comrades, called 'the volunteers', were ready to starve and be captured. They were ready to die. They had already given up their lives for the freedom and independence of our country. On the day the news of this decision arrived, the comrades started singing in their most powerful voices, with joy and a sense of pride and vigour.

---

34 In fact, Angola only gained its independence on 11 November 1975.

This was their song:

Afulika alishe konyala	The whole of Africa is nearly
Ola manguluka	Independent
Kakele kaNamibia	except Namibia
NaZimbabwe	and Zimbabwe
NaSouth Afulika	and South Africa

   (Chorus)

Oyo ombili yetu	This is our peace
Oyo Enyanyu kufye	This is our happiness
Twanyanyukwa ngele tuli mopaati yetu	We are joyful to be in our party
Otwa waana twapwa	We feel contented

Nakada, Mbulunganga,	Nakada, Mbulunganga,
Haulyondjaba	Haulyondjaba
Komaanda ovakwaita	Give orders to the combatants
Shaashi efimbo lapwapo	because time has run out
Fye otwa hala	We want
Tukanwe mokahonde	to taste (enemy) blood

   (Chorus)

Vakwaita amushe voPULANA	PLAN[35] combatants, all of you
Kwateni komahomato	hold onto your ammunition
Kufeni oGerendeP	take the GrandP
NoBazooka	and Bazooka
Mota nai komande	The mortars shall give the command

   (Chorus)

---

35 People's Liberation Army of Namibia (PLAN) was SWAPO's military wing.

There were about fifteen of these 'volunteers', amongst them were Matias Ndakolo (popularly known as Mbulunganga), Paulus Nandenga (Zulu), Wilbard Tashiya Shikolo (Nakada), Elise Haulyondjaba, John Hamukoto (Kalola), Jonas Kataleonga (Katengela), Erickson Hauwanga (Kapanya), Jonas Kapapu (Mumbwela Weemhadi), Linus Hamwele (Mawila), Sakeus Kapulwa (Kapuleko) and Ismail Kamati (Ngiringiri). I cannot remember the names of the others. So, Nakada, Mbulunganga, Haulyondjaba and Zulu left for Angola with a large contingent of very well-trained, well-armed and dedicated freedom fighters to try and establish a northern front.

We admired these comrades for taking the heroic decision to undertake this mission, which they knew from experience was a difficult one. At that time, SWAPO did not have any logistical or infrastructural support in Angola. These men knew that it would be difficult, even impossible, for them to get food and water. They knew that their way to Namibia through Angola would be hard, and may well cost them their lives. Yet Angola was a very strategic support base or springboard for our fighters to cross through into Namibia.

Angola was not yet independent, and the Portuguese government there would not give our comrades a friendly welcome. Apart from this, there were three liberation movements in Angola fighting their own battles against the Portuguese colonial forces.[36] Our comrades knew that they might be caught in the crossfire. You can just imagine what might happen when three liberation movements are fighting for the independence of one country. Although there was no formal, open hostility between them, each had a different political orientation. There was competition amongst them because they were political rivals competing for popularity to win the hearts and minds of the Angolan people. So there was much pushing and pulling, which culminated in a long and entangled armed conflict between the two stronger movements, MPLA and UNITA.

---

36 These were the National Union for the Total Independence of Angola (UNITA), the Popular Movement for the Liberation of Angola (MPLA) and the National Liberation Front of Angola (FNLA).

This group of combatants made it to Angola successfully, and while they were looking for a way out of Angola to Namibia, the Portuguese colonial government surrendered. It looked as though Angola was well on its way to independence. The ceasefire was declared so that the three liberation movements could prepare themselves for national elections. However, the sudden departure of the Portuguese colonial regime, together with the absence of a transitional government, left a governance vacuum in the country. Each of the liberation movements felt that they had the right to rule Angola and to take charge of the country. There was no neutral mediator to oversee the Angolan election process and the transition to independence. A conflict therefore developed between the three movements, which resulted in a civil war that lasted for twenty-six years.

This conflict caused big challenges for the SWAPO leadership because it had freedom fighters who were trained and ready to take up arms but who were stranded in Angola. Our combatants wanted to go to the war zone and fight for our independence, but as you can imagine this was no easy task as the passage to Namibia was full of obstacles. When they walked through Angola, they went through some territories that were controlled by UNITA and others that were controlled by the MPLA. When hostilities developed, it became very difficult for them to avoid becoming entangled in the internal conflict, and to explain their neutrality.

The other problem our leadership faced was that they had combatants in camps in Tanzania and Zambia who had returned from military schools in other countries and were ready for combat, yet there was no clear passage for them to get to Namibia. These men were infused with high morale and did not have the patience to stay in the camps. They were eagerly awaiting orders to go to the war zone to fight for our independence. It was difficult to keep these forceful young men at Kongwa. Our leaders had to think hard to come up with activities to keep them busy and occupied with something they would consider useful. Just imagine Kongwa filled with trained combatants sitting around in someone else's country without a job to do. How would you go about controlling their activities and movement? So, our leaders did not have an easy task.

Imagine this too – here we were at Kongwa in Tanzania, a country that was once a colony just like Namibia but which had fought for and won its independence. We had been told this time and again and were inspired and motivated to fight for our freedom and independence too, just like other people in the world. Even the Bible said that what is free on earth would be free in heaven. So, what would happen to those of us who were enslaved on earth? What place would we go to when we got to heaven?

Leading people in an armed liberation struggle was complex and complicated. Due to this complexity, a decision was never right or wrong. Much later, around April 1974, following political change in Portugal after the government was overthrown,[37] a group of about seven fighters were again sent to Angola. Amongst them were Commander Dimo Hamaambo, Aaron Embashu (Shongambele), Thomas Komati and Hamunyela waShalale. I cannot remember the others by name.

******

Soon after we had said goodbye to the fifteen 'volunteers', another group of comrades began preparing to leave for the Soviet Union to undergo military training. We were all informed that we would be sent for advanced military training. I was supposed to go with my male comrades to the Soviet Union, but when the list of names arrived from Dar es Salaam, mine was not on it. All my male comrades went for further training to Ghana, Egypt or the Soviet Union, while I remained at Kongwa.

I realised that all the people with whom I had left Namibia were leaving Kongwa for further training, while I remained behind. Even Shikongo shaHangala went to the Soviet Union alongside other comrades. People who came to Kongwa for military training were sent to the war zone and found me still at Kongwa on their return. I do not know why I was left off the list. Perhaps there were no military training

---

37 A reference to the Carnation Revolution, a military coup which began in Lisbon on 25 April 1974. The government was overthrown and Portugal began withdrawing from its African colonies.

facilities for women in the countries to which my male comrades were sent. It could not have been because I was illiterate as I did know the alphabet and had basic literacy and numeracy, albeit in my mother tongue. If this had been an issue, there would have been many people left off the list. I was a fully trained combatant and was ready for advanced military training. I was also ready to face combat. This day never came. I remained at Kongwa.

I could not just sit about idle; I had to find things to do to keep me busy on a daily basis. As I was part of the camp leadership, I had my share of leadership issues to deal with. Apart from this, I started assisting *Tate* Peter Haitembu (Shinyafa) and *Tate* Kalangula to manage the clinic. I received some first aid training and took responsibility for dispensing medicine and treating minor ailments, such as headaches and fever. We did not have many medical supplies, just a few painkillers such as paracetamol and aspirin, anti-malaria tablets such as quinine and chloroquine, and a few antibiotics such as penicillin and tetracycline.

******

During our stay at Kongwa no one, other than SWAPO members, was allowed to visit us in the camp. We could leave the camp, however, to visit Tanzanian family members. However, leaving the camp was only allowed on Saturdays and Sundays. It was done on request and in turns. We were soldiers and had a responsibility to our host country and to the cause for which we were fighting. Therefore, we could not afford to all go out at once to visit our Tanzanian friends and leave the camp empty. We made camp rules by which all of us had to abide. We regulated our conduct and imposed self-discipline. These rules included our various responsibilities toward our host country, especially regarding our behaviour when we visited the local shops and places of leisure.

The people of Tanzania welcomed us in their country. They were sympathetic towards our independence struggle. They were friendly and treated us with humility and compassion. My memory of the Tanzanian people is a pleasant one, and this is what I carried with me even after independence. They were our friends in our time of need. They accepted us in the true spirit of solidarity and comradeship. They showed us true love and made an effort to understand who we were, why we were in their country, and what we were fighting for. They understood that we were freedom fighters and that we were undergoing military training in order to go and fight for the independence of our country so that we too could be free. During this period I could not speak English. The local people spoke to us in their language, Swahili. As a result, I started learning Swahili, and after about three months was able to speak it like a native speaker.

The Tanzanians would organise social functions for us Namibians. They cooked a lot of food and invited us as guests of honour into their communities and homes. These social get-togethers were called 'Mama Rosa'. I also had a good friend who used to invite me over to her house on the weekends. Oh, I was treated like a queen. I loved chicken – even today it is my favourite food. My Tanzanian friends got to know this, and chicken dishes were specially cooked for me. One time, they slaughtered a whole goat for me.

Many of us Namibians were Christians and wanted to go to church on Sundays. We had no church at Kongwa so we often went to the local church service, where we were made to feel welcome. People were curious and often asked where our other women were, and why they did not also come to church. In time they realised, with some shock, that I was the only woman in the camp, amongst hundreds of men. They used to ask jokingly of my male comrades, 'Don't you have women in Namibia? Why is there only one woman in your camp? Is she truly Namibian or have you stolen her from somewhere?'

I had arrived at Kongwa in 1965 with the first intake of trainees and I remained there for nine years, until 1974, when our leadership told me that I was overqualified as a military combatant and that it was time for me to move on to Zambia, where the party would give me new assignments. So I left Kongwa for Lusaka.

MOTHER

4

ZAMBIA

I had been in Lusaka for about a week when the SWAPO officials told me that I would be taken to the Old Farm, a farm on the outskirts of Lusaka. I was told that there were Namibian women and children staying there who had recently arrived from home and who needed my support urgently. I happily joined them.

I had expected the Old Farm to look like Kongwa, but to my astonishment I found men, women, youth and children at the camp. Oh, I was pleasantly surprised. For several years I had been the only woman amongst men; suddenly, I was in the midst of about fifteen fellow women from my country. They were living at the camp while their husbands were away for military training, or fighting the war. This was a great joy. We got to know one another. Seemingly, the women had already been told who I was. The Old Farm leadership told them in my presence that I had come to give them orientation about SWAPO and to help them adjust to life in the camps. The name Mukwahepo followed me to Zambia. Everyone at the Old Farm called me this. The only difference was that at the Old Farm my name was modified to *Meekulu* (Grandmother) Mukwahepo. Even people who were older than me called me this. I had found a new home amongst my fellow Namibians.

Amongst the women at the Old Farm were MaGeorge, MaBrown and BoMagret. During the struggle, we were not very keen to ask our comrades for details about who they were and what village they came from. The majority of these women were from the Caprivi, in the extreme northeast of Namibia. They spoke mainly Subia and Silozi languages. About three of them came from the Okavango (also in the northeast of Namibia) and they spoke Rukwangali. The rest of the women were from Owambo (in northern Namibia) and spoke the Oshiwambo languages.

I was overjoyed to be living amongst my fellow countrywomen, and felt so proud that they had taken the decision to join the liberation struggle. I felt invigorated. During all the years I had lived in Tanzania, I had not seen many Namibians. I had only heard stories that the war in Angola had intensified and that in Namibia the situation had become critical, and many people had died. I had been in a war zone during my travels through Angola. I had seen that war kills people, so I worried a lot about people back home and how they were surviving the war.

My spirit was revived when I saw these women. They restored my hope of seeing my own family one day, once we had gained our independence. Some of the women had small children who became infected with measles, which is a very contagious disease. The camp leadership were worried about the spread of the infection and decided that BoMagret and I should take the sick children to the hospital in Lusaka and stay there with them until they were completely well again. Being the lastborn in my family, I had not had any direct experience nursing sick children. I had grown up in my uncle's house where there were no small children. I was always the youngest one in the house. (There was not a single child at Kongwa, although we saw a lot of children when we went to the village to visit Tanzanian families.) I had no children of my own. So, I had to learn how to take care of children at that point in my adult life, in Lusaka, when I was asked by SWAPO to take care of the sick children at the Old Farm.

Taking care of the sick children was a bit tough at first, but I learnt quickly by watching how the mothers handled their children. I soon began to understand the children and could respond to their needs. We remained at the state hospital in Lusaka for about a month. The doctors discharged the children as soon as they had recovered, and we returned the well children to their mothers at the Old Farm. We then returned to the hospital with more sick children. I was very pleased when all the children who had been infected with measles had recovered and had been returned to their parents in good health. The Zambian government paid for all the medical costs incurred. Once the measles epidemic was over, we returned to the Old Farm.

In 1974, there was an exodus of people – young and old, men and women, boys and girls – from Namibia to Zambia. They had come to join the struggle. We wanted them to feel welcome, so we tried our best to look after them and teach them how to survive in the camps. Our camp commanders at the time were Comrades Benjamin Namalambo and Aaron Shihepo. Amongst the groups who had arrived from home were teenagers. Our leadership had realised that some of them were too young to go for military training and therefore decided to call upon the educationists within SWAPO to design a school programme for the Namibian children at the Old Farm. Comrades Nahas Angula and Festus November Mthoko were responsible for education. Dr Libertina Amathila was responsible for health education, along with establishing health facilities at the camp. Comrade Aaron Shihepo oversaw the administration and management of the camp.

MaGeorge and I were responsible for the nutritional wellbeing of the babies and young children. We established a small kitchen that catered for their needs. The children lived with their parents, mainly their mothers, but were brought to the children's kitchen three times a day to be fed. In the morning we gave them porridge, while at lunchtime and in the evening we cooked mainly fish and occasionally meat.

Although we had both heard about each other when we were in Tanzania, it was only at the Old Farm, in 1974, that I met Dr Libertina Amathila for the first time. Dr Amathila was very happy to meet me and wanted to get closer to me. She therefore took me away from the children and reassigned me to the clinic, where I was to take care of clinic hygiene and distribute essentials to patients and the elderly. I did not mind these tasks as I was already familiar with this kind of work from the clinic at Kongwa. I was responsible for changing and washing the clinic bedding, tablecloths and curtains. We did not have washing machines, so I washed everything by hand in a big basin. When we experienced a water shortage at the Old Farm, I took my laundry to the riverside and washed it there. We did not have many patients, so the work was manageable. I was also responsible for washing those patients who were too weak or sick to wash themselves. I was young, healthy and full of energy.

******

At the beginning of 1975, we were relocated from the Old Farm to a new place called Nyango in the Kaoma District in Western Province, Zambia. Everyone in the entire camp moved. We took with us all our movable health, education and administration equipment. On the day we arrived at Nyango, I accidentally injured my thumb when my hand was squashed between two huge poles during the construction of our new home. Dr Amathila took me to the nearest Zambian hospital, a trip of about twelve kilometres on foot, there and back. I felt really proud to know her. She was a well-educated woman, and also a humble, down-to-earth and very caring person who was devoted and passionate when it came to serving the needs of others. She was the kind of person you wanted close to you when you were sick and vulnerable. Dr Amathila was always full of life. She was also a very practical woman who could do anything – when we were cooking, she was there; when we were constructing our shelters, she was there. She was a happy person, approachable even by children, and ever full of energy.

In the whole of SWAPO, we had two medical doctors; namely, Dr Iyambo Indongo and Dr Libertina Amathila. These doctors had a huge responsibility taking care of the health of every SWAPO member in exile. SWAPO had several civilian camps in Angola, Zambia and Zaire.[38] Every SWAPO camp had its own clinic or hospital. Our two doctors had to see to it that the established medical centres were functional, that they were managed professionally, and that they had a reasonable medical stock. With the support of nurses, these two doctors ran our medical facilities until 1978, when SWAPO received medical doctors from Sweden, Finland and later the German Democratic Republic (GDR) to run some of our hospitals and clinics, specifically those in Kwanza-Sul and Lubango in Angola.

Due to my thumb injury, I was no longer able to do the laundry for our clinic at Nyango. Instead, Dr Amathila made me responsible for cleaning the hospital and providing support to the elderly people in the camp. I was responsible for bringing them water and helping them to wash themselves and their clothing in order to ensure that their personal and living environment remained hygienic. When there was

---

38 The Belgian Congo gained its independence in 1960, becoming known as the Congo. In 1971, the name of the country was changed to Zaire, until 1997, when it became the Democratic Republic of the Congo. Mukwahepo refers to it as the Congo.

a general distribution of provisions to all camp residents, such as food, soap, Vaseline, clothing or blankets, it was my responsibility to collect the elderly people's share and deliver it to them in person.

* * * * * *

Becoming involved with children was not something I had planned. I do not think anyone had planned it. It happened because, as the Nyango camp grew in size, more responsibilities were added to my list. Apart from cleaning the hospital and taking care of the elderly, I was made responsible for any child who was born with complications, or any mother who suffered after birth. Taking care of children and young mothers became more and more demanding, and eventually required all my energy. Other comrades therefore took over my various responsibilities, while I focused solely on looking after small children, some of whom came to me a few hours after they were born.

Our nurses were very well trained and had a true love for their profession. They took great care of their patients. They were not paid for their service and yet their dedication to duty was the highest I have ever seen. Dr Amathila was an excellent organiser. She was also a good mother. She worked tirelessly and managed our hospital competently. She was exemplary in her leadership and inspired all the nurses because she was forever on the move. I am very proud of her.

One day, I was urgently called to go and help out at the hospital. When I arrived, the nurses told me that a young woman had given birth smoothly to a very healthy baby girl but had suffered severe postnatal trauma. I was told that the baby was healthy but that the mother was very ill, to the extent that she was unstable and could not look after her baby. She was hallucinating and uttering disjointed sentences. She was also eagerly removing her clothes. Our hospital authorities then sent her to a hospital in Lusaka for treatment.

I was given the responsibility of looking after this newborn baby, under the close observation of the hospital authorities. I therefore took over the mother's bed. The nurses gave me food for the baby and instructions as to when and how to feed her. They explained in great detail that mother's milk is the most crucial nourishment for a baby, especially during the first three months, because it is full of the vitamins, minerals and antibodies necessary to build up a baby and protect it from ailments. As this baby had not been breastfed at all, she may have acquired nutritional deficiencies and may not have been easily able to resist illnesses. The nurses emphasised that I should take extra hygienic precautions and care when feeding, bathing and generally handling this vulnerable baby. At first this seemed like an impossible task, but we were lucky to watch the baby grow and become a week old, then a month. At that point, the baby and I were discharged from the hospital. Proudly, I took her home.

The hospital provided the baby with all the food they could under the difficult circumstances of war. This was mainly baby milk and baby porridge. The father of the baby was a very responsible man – at the time of his baby's birth he was a student at the United Nations Institute for Namibia (UNIN) in Lusaka. He also helped to buy food for his baby. Sometimes, he even sent us money so that we could buy ourselves necessary household items. This baby marked a turning point in my permanent assignments working with children in the SWAPO camps.

The Nyango camp was very busy, with more and more people arriving almost every week from Namibia to join SWAPO in exile. Our population increased tremendously. When people arrived from home, they were received and then interviewed so that SWAPO could determine important information about them. If a person had been a teacher in Namibia, that person was assigned the role of teaching the children at Nyango. If the person was a nurse, he or she may have been sent for military training to become a combat nurse, or assigned to take care of the health needs of the comrades at the front or in the battlefields. SWAPO looked at people and their potential to undergo military training so that they could join PLAN to become combatants and be sent to the war to face the enemy. Not everyone who joined SWAPO became a member of PLAN.

When young people joined SWAPO in exile, many had left their parents back home in Namibia. SWAPO took over the parenting role and looked after them all. As there were so many young people arriving from Namibia, it was necessary to begin a vigorous education programme. SWAPO began looking for teachers amongst its adult members and brought them to Old Farm and later to Nyango to teach the children. Comrades Lineekela Hailundu Kalenga, Nahas Angula and Festus November Mthoko would be able to tell you all about the pioneering work they did in education in the camps; how they developed and implemented the school curriculum. Also, the SWAPO leadership and members of the diplomatic missions were very busy soliciting support – such as food, medical supplies, blankets, educational materials and books for our schools, building materials, clothing, soap and Vaseline – for Nyango from all over the world. SWAPO also actively sought scholarships from friendly governments and peoples of the world to send young Namibians to school. We in SWAPO believed strongly that independence was coming and that, when we liberated our country, we would need educated people to run the government. For this reason, SWAPO prioritised its education programme and considered studying to be one of its most important activities. When these young people completed their studies, they returned to the camps. SWAPO then reassigned them to those areas of endeavour that best advanced the interests of the struggle.

Some small children travelled from Namibia with their parents; others were born at Nyango. The SWAPO education programme offered opportunities to every able Namibian to go and study. Any young person with a child older than two years of age was entitled to go to school abroad. The difficulties of going to study abroad with a small child were taken into consideration – especially the problem of childcare during study hours – and a strong social network was set up, particularly among the female elders in the camps, to provide motherly care and support to children whilst their parents were away studying. SWAPO students were sent all over the world, even to countries with which we did not share a common language. That is why many Namibians speak Russian, English, French, Swahili, Swedish, Finnish, German, Spanish, Chinese and other languages. Another issue, therefore, was that if these students had taken their children along when they went to study, the children would have had difficulties finding other children to play with due to the language barrier. So, leaving the children at Nyango camp under the care of the elderly women was considered the best solution. Although this was not always a smooth ride, it was a solution that worked.

This was how it came about that some of our young comrades asked me to take their children into my home to look after them while they were away furthering their education. Apart from asking a comrade to look after their children, people also had the option of leaving them in the SWAPO kindergarten. The young people were very mobile, and moving children from one person to another was not always in the best interests of the child. We, the older ones, provided more stable long-term care. For instance, there was the case of a young comrade who had left her child in the care of a friend in order to take up a scholarship to study abroad but, before she had even left Lusaka, news reached her that her friend had also been offered a scholarship to study abroad.

At Nyango camp, I realised that I was not getting any younger. I had missed out on the opportunity to go to school during my youth. I realised that I was surrounded by mothers who, although they had babies, were still young enough to take up the challenge of going to school. Some teenagers fell pregnant – children having children. As the eldest of the inhabitants of Nyango, I took it upon myself to teach these very young mothers how to take care of their babies, and played the role of both mother and grandmother. Even though I had no children of my own, these young mothers looked to me as *meme*. In fact, it was at Nyango that the young mothers started calling me *Meme* Mukwahepo, while their children called me *Meekulu* Mukwahepo. Many people who knew me from Nyango, and later from Kwanza-Sul, had no idea what my real name was because throughout the struggle I was always called *Meekulu* Mukwahepo.

I felt duty bound to give advice to my young comrades, advice which their biological mothers would have given them had they been in Namibia. These young mothers were not homogeneous. They reacted in different ways to pregnancy and childbirth, and supporting them required multiple skills. For instance, there were cases where a mother gave birth to a very healthy child but had no milk with which to feed it. Or where a mother gave birth to a healthy child but was unhealthy herself. In these cases, the camp authorities would be eager for me to take care of both the mother and the child, and would assist me by giving me baby food whenever possible.

Some of the young mothers failed completely to learn how to take care of their own children. No matter what training we gave them, they just could not cope with motherly responsibility. I had cases of young mothers coming to my home and staying on and on with their babies until eventually I took over the care of the baby. I gladly accepted the babies, especially when they were given to me before they became undernourished. Sometimes, I was given babies who were tired and undernourished. They had tiny bodies, fragile skin and big stomachs. I fed those babies day and night until they were healthy, but I preferred to be given babies who were in good condition.

In contrast to the above cases, there were some young mothers who had a natural love for their babies and took great care of them. They would do everything in their power to make sure that their babies were always clean and neatly dressed. Yet even in these positive circumstances, where the young mothers accepted the joy of motherhood, my support was still needed because they did not have the experience of raising children. For instance, they always carried their babies on their backs, or put them down on a mat or a bed, but never on the floor. They were afraid that their babies would get dirty or catch germs if they were put down on the floor.

Those of us who were giving this early childhood support noticed that some one-year-olds whose mothers we were supporting could not crawl or walk, while the children we were raising were usually crawling by about six months and walking before a year. I realised we were paying too much attention to issues such as hygiene and feeding, and not enough to the development of the children. Important life skills, such as learning to get around by crawling or walking, came naturally when an enabling environment was created. The children of inexperienced mothers could not crawl or walk because they were being carried on their mother's back all the time, or being placed on a mat or a bed. I began holding individual and group sessions with the mothers to explain how children acquire the basic life skills of crawling, walking and moving their bodies so that they develop properly. Eventually, the message got through, and the concept 'teach one, teach all' became a reality.

******

I loved this work. I was doing it for the community, but I was also doing it for myself. These children gave me a family, they gave me love. When they looked at me, they looked at their mother and grandmother. After having witnessed the tragedy of children dying during the war in Nambuangongo in Angola during our journey into exile, it hurt me so much to see children suffer in any way. What was required of me at Nyango was a willingness to serve these children, and to help the young mothers to take good care of them.

Apart from the sense of duty I felt to play the role of mother to these young mothers and their children, I was also inspired to set up what was an important social network system. When the parents of these children went to study further or to fight in the war, all the children had was us. We supplied the crucial parental relationships they needed. Many of these children did not even know their absent parents – they only knew us, the old ones who looked after them. If you asked one of them,

'Who is your mother?'

'Mukwahepo,' the child would reply.

If you asked further, 'Who is your father?'

'Mukwahepo.'

I was totally shocked when I heard these replies for the first time. I considered it my fault that these children thought I was their mother or father and did not know the names of their parents. I therefore made them repeat their parents' names over and over, and explained to them why they were not with us in the camps. I told them stories of our young men and women who were fighting bravely at the battlefront for our country's independence. I told them about other young comrades who were studying hard abroad; how education was important because after independence we would need educated people to run the affairs of our government. This did not help much, as these children continued thinking and believing that I, Mukwahepo, was both their mother and father.

The children made my life truly worthwhile. They gave me pure love and taught me how to become a friend to children. With my children I never felt lonely. They were good entertainers – I had sore stomach muscles from laughing at them all the time! Sometimes, I just sat amongst them and watched them play, sing and dance. They filled my heart with joy.

The children were also very curious. They wanted to know and learn things. Whenever I went somewhere with them, they were forever asking what, why, when, where and who. I realised they were asking questions because they needed clarity. So, I explained things to them until they understood. I tried to do this whenever they asked me something, because children do not usually repeat their questions. When I explained something to a child, I always tried to be truthful, even in difficult situations, because often I would hear that child explain the same thing in a similar manner to the next child.

Providing information to the children was important. Even when they asked questions that seemed silly, I tried to reply patiently and truthfully. I also explained to the children that when they saw me talking to another adult they should not bother me but leave us to finish our conversation, unless it was something very important. I tried to teach them these and other important life skills in order to help form their characters. It was alright for them to come and announce, '*Meekulu*, I have something very important to tell you.' The children enjoyed coming to whisper things in my ear whenever I was busy with someone else.

Some of the children were very lucky because their parents were studying under generous scholarships that allowed them to come for a holiday to Nyango every second year. Also, some parents who had studied teaching were posted to teach at the SWAPO Education Centres after graduating, so were reunited with their children. This provided an excellent opportunity for the children to be with their biological parents. Usually, I did not allow the returning parents to stay with me for too long because I was concerned about the impact their presence would have on the other children living with me whose parents had no opportunity to visit them. I was lucky in that all the parents whose children were under my care were understanding of the circumstances, and when they returned from school for good, or for the holidays, they tried to treat all the children they found with me equally. They returned with a lot of nice things for the children, yet if they gave something to their own child, they also gave something to the other children. This was very good, because then all the children felt happy about the visitor.

Often, returning young parents had it tough because many of the children did not easily accept them as parents. The parents, on the other hand, looked forward to reuniting with their children. Usually, when they came for holidays or retuned for good from studying, they would come and live with me. I would then call the child and say, 'Here is your father (or mother).' I would tell the child the name of the parent and where he or she had come from. In some cases, children ran happily to their parents, especially boys. Smaller children between the ages of two and five easily accepted their parents, compared to the older ones. This rejection of parents by their children was difficult for everyone. Nevertheless, we managed it.

Then there was another category of children – those who had been born in Namibia during the struggle and were left in the camps by their parents, who then went to study further, or went to the front. This was a difficult group to deal with. There were times when we found them singing:

'Meme afiyange ndee tai natate okwalond ehaulala
(Mother left me while my father climbed the army truck)

Meme afiyange haivele, outate nonghenda keikwete'
(Mother left me sick, father had no pity)

I must say that I was shocked to hear this, and realised that we had not opened up enough to the children so they could understand the absence of their biological parents in their lives. This was a big concern to all of us who worked with the children. So, we discussed the matter and took it further to our camp commander to outline a strategy for helping to relieve the children's disappointment. It was decided in a meeting that I should talk to the affected children on an individual basis, one by one by one, to hear what was eating them up. I was therefore a self-trained psychologist in the camp. Usually, I could calm an angry person down, or motivate someone whose morale was low. I did not go to school to study these things. They came to me through life experience.

My greatest asset is good listening skills. Listening is a very important life skill, especially for people who work with children. Every child I have met in my life has been unique. Children's natures differ. Some children are shy and have difficulty expressing themselves in front of adults. So, they go round and round talking rubbish before they warm up and say what they really meant to tell you. Patience is the key to working successfully with children. If a person has no patience, I cannot imagine how that person can function amongst children and young people. You need patience when you listen to children, to help them overcome the fear of making themselves heard. If you stop them abruptly by butting in every time they are talking, you may destroy their confidence and make them introverted or aggressive.

I spoke to the children with the above issues in mind. Fortunately, most did not have many problems except for the fact that they missed their biological parents, especially those whose parents had gone to study. The children wanted to know why their parents had not taken them along. We had to explain that they had gone to study abroad on a scholarship that only made provision for one person. Their parents could not take them along because they would have no one to look after them whilst they studied, day and night. In some of the countries where the parents went to study, languages other than English were spoken. We explained that if their parents had taken them along, they would have been lonely because there would be no common language with which to communicate with the children of those countries.

A further issue was that the children did not understand what it meant for their parents to go to study in Scandinavia, China or the United Kingdom, and how that differed from a person going to teach at a school in Nyango. The children saw other children in the camp leaving with their parents, especially the children of teachers, nurses and other adults who provided critical services to the camp residents. They would then ask, for instance, '*Meekulu*, why is Tuyeni leaving with her *meme*, but not me? Because Tuyeni's *meme* is also going to school?' Also, we were in a war situation and the children had their own understanding of the impact of this on their lives in exile.

It was our duty to explain all of this to the children. We would say, 'Your parents are busy studying. They have no time to run around making friends for you. It is best that you are here, with friends to play with. Your parents love you very much, but they have made a huge personal sacrifice for the struggle. They have gone to study to become educated so that, when independence comes, we will have educated people to run the government and economy of our country. I know many of you whose fathers have gone to the war to fight in order to liberate our country from colonialism, so that we can all return home to an independent Namibia and have happy lives with our families.'

We told them that their parents were fulfilling a very important role doing SWAPO work, and that they should all be very proud of them. We said that they had not abandoned them or neglected them. 'No, they are on duty, and we here are also on duty to look after you. We are your mothers, your fathers and your grandmothers. SWAPO sent us here just for you. It breaks my heart to hear you say that they abandoned you. You are not unwanted. You have not been denied or rejected. You are the sons and daughters of very brave SWAPO cadres, studying hard for the future of our country, and fighting bravely for our freedom and independence.'

So, we had to face the children and talk to them in order to understand the reasons for their reactions. But before we talked to them, we had to try to understand their fears and their worries. We were very careful, and measured every word we said to them, especially because we wanted to be truthful and open. We met regularly to share our experiences and advise one another about how to talk to the children. We needed to explain the struggle to them so that they could build up their own understanding of the war situation. We decided to talk to them as a group. We did not write down what we said to them, but basically, this is what we told them:

'We are Namibians, from Namibia. We have come to Zambia to escape colonialism and apartheid. Our country is not free, like Zambia. Our people are in bondage. They are not free to rule themselves, to speak or decide things for themselves, or to participate in governing their country. They are not treated as citizens in their own country, but as slaves. We want independence, freedom and justice for all Namibians. We want to rule ourselves and to run the affairs of our country. Our colonisers are ruling our country by force, and when we ask questions, or dare to challenge the authority of the colonial government, we are arrested, beaten up, put in jail and even killed. Like ourselves, your parents took a decision to join SWAPO, our liberation movement, in exile in order to organise ourselves to fight and liberate our country, instead of suffering oppression in silence at home in Namibia. We also realise that after our liberation we will need educated people to run our country's affairs, and this is why we send people to study and further their education in other countries.'

After these open talks, the children's understanding improved drastically and we were relieved to see them make peace with the situation and with their biological parents. Although I cannot claim complete success in this regard, as children are children, and new challenges occur all the time as they grow up. We continued guiding and explaining things to them when necessary. We never punished them but tried to make them see where their behaviour was inappropriate, and how to avoid making a mistake twice. We never reported children to the camp authorities for disciplinary action. We used a soft approach to raise them ourselves.

******

Nyango was not the only civilian camp SWAPO had in exile. Like Nyango in Zambia, Cassinga was a settlement for the SWAPO civilian population in southern Angola. Most of its inhabitants were women, children, young adults, elderly people and the sick. On 4 May 1978, the South African Defence Force (SADF) attacked Cassinga, and many innocent people were killed in cold blood. From this experience, the SWAPO leadership learnt the hard way that the South African apartheid regime intended to target their civilian camps with military aggression and kill all Namibians in exile, whether they were PLAN members or civilians. So, as it was SWAPO's policy to protect human lives, the leadership took a decision to establish PLAN military bases around all the camps which housed its civilian population in exile, to provide its civilians with security and to defend them against this enemy aggression. As a result, PLAN members had to split their efforts between fighting to liberate Namibia and defending the civilian camps in Angola and Zambia.

The Nyango camp, one of the oldest settlements for the SWAPO civilian population in exile, was established in 1974. One day, in August 1979, we heard our own artillery being fired. We looked up to see several military bomber planes flying over our camp. It was difficult to count the exact number of planes because they were flying round and round, and we did not know whether they were the same planes coming round again or different ones. There seemed to be about four of them. Although it was not clear to us what was going on, we immediately thought they were SADF military bomber planes. We did not know whether their intention was to bomb us or just to frighten and intimidate us. We thought it could well be that they were using psychological warfare on the SWAPO leadership by showing them that they were capable of repeating at Nyango what they had done at Cassinga.

It was fortunate that, on that winter's day, the SADF had found the Nyango camp under the protection of PLAN, unlike at Cassinga where they had found the civilians without military defence. Our protectors were the first to spot the planes and ascertain that they were indeed enemy warplanes. They therefore opened fire on them. We had heard the artillery shots even before the sound of the planes. The firing of the shots caused the planes to leave without having dropped a single bomb on us. They never came back to Nyango again.

Our PLAN combatants were on the alert at all times, armed to the teeth and ready to counter the enemy at any moment. They were very serious about their duty; totally committed and dedicated to protecting and defending the lives of those at Nyango. All their energy and thoughts were about fulfilling this duty. They undertook their role bravely and with a sense of fierce pride. PLAN combatants were strictly disciplined, motivated and determined regarding their mission. They had high moral values and were infused with the spirit of unity. Therefore, the residents of Nyango felt totally secure; that their lives were in good and responsible hands.

These PLAN combatants did not live with us. Their military bases were located on the outskirts of Nyango camp. We did not visit them at their bases, we never went there, but we sometimes saw them walking through Nyango when they came to undertake whatever military inspections were necessary. The camp had its own commander, Comrade Wilbardt Shipweya Iyambo, popularly known as Willie. The PLAN combatants had their own commander, Comrade Frans Kapofi.

******

When our camp commander saw the enemy warplanes flying round and round our camp and realised that our PLAN combatants had already opened fire on them, he started to evacuate the residents into the forest, beginning with the children, the ill and the disabled. I retreated from the camp with the small children who were under my care. Everyone was hastily evacuated. As soon as we had left the camp, the PLAN combatants moved in. The point of this was that if the enemy had returned with the intention of bombing and destroying the camp, at least the civilians would have been gone. The combatants would have been ready to face and confront the enemy.

There were a lot of people living at Nyango, although it is difficult to estimate the civilian population because it was never static. There was always movement of people coming and going. During Christmas and New Year, for example, the population was at its highest – about five thousand people. But if you were to come to Nyango in February, for example, you would have only found about three to four thousand inhabitants. This was because some comrades who were working or studying at various institutions in Zambia often came home to Nyango to enjoy the end-of-year holidays with their comrades and families.

Also, many of them had children at the kindergarten at Nyango, so the holidays provided an opportunity for them to be with their loved ones. Therefore, one can roughly estimate the population of Nyango at any given time to vary between three to five thousand people, depending on the time of the year.

At the time of this attempted bombing in 1979, there were over one thousand adults and about three thousand small children and teenagers living at Nyango. It was therefore quite a challenge for the camp authorities to provide shelter and logistical support to so many people during the two week retreat into the forest. In spite of this, we brought the situation under control and managed the crisis well under the circumstances.

******

Many of the children at Nyango camp at the time of this incident were terrified by the possibility of being attacked. Their eyes and faces were full of anxiety, and some of them lost their appetite. They asked us what would happen if the warplanes came back to bomb our camp. I, too, had fears and worries about being attacked, but of course I could not voice them to the children. I could not even discuss my worries with the other adults in the camp because they looked to me for inspiration. The children were more open than the adults, and felt free to speak their minds. When they had a problem, they spoke out about it. If their spirits were low, you could see this by their appearance. The adults tried to boost their morale by telling them funny stories that made them laugh, or stories that took their minds off thoughts of a possible attack. Although we could not rule out this possibility because we were at war with our colonisers, we assured the children that our PLAN combatants were ever ready to face the enemy and defend us all. We tried very hard to keep the children active and busy – playing, singing and dancing – to keep them from worrying about the war.

I used to tell the children traditional stories; fairy tales that had been told to us as children by our parents. I told them stories in the evenings until they fell asleep. Even when I saw that they were very tired and ready for bed, I still called them. 'Children, children, come, let me tell you a story.' Then they all gathered around me. The small ones always came to sit on my lap. And so the stories would begin. They listened attentively. It always amazed me how fast these children learnt things. I would tell them a story once and, the next time, they were the ones retelling me the same story. Sometimes, they would tell me a different story that they had heard from another person.

We also taught them things that had to do with self-protection and the survival of all the camp residents. For instance, we taught them that lighting a fire in the open was dangerous, especially at night, because the smoke could be seen by the enemy spy planes, which would give away our hiding place and make it easy for the enemy to attack us. We told the children to avoid going to the river alone and to be careful of all strangers because the colour and form of the enemy could not be predicted.

The small children demanded a lot more attention, love and care, but they were easier to talk to, unlike the school-going children who were a real challenge. Most of the children of school-going age understood the war situation and demanded to go and join the armed struggle. When we asked them to go into the forest and hide from the enemy, they told us point blank that they did not want to stay in the camps to run and hide like women and children. This was especially the case with the boys. They did not easily follow our instructions. It took a lot of talking and convincing to make them understand that this was the right thing for all of us to do. They asked us straightforward questions. 'We are men and are ready to go to the war. Why do you keep us in the camps, like children and old people? Instead of letting us go to join PLAN, you want us to run around and hide from other men's bullets, as if we were women. You are wasting our struggle time by keeping us here.'

It was our duty as adults and guardians to these children to ensure that everyone was evacuated from the camp. Luckily, our camp commander, Comrade Willie Iyambo, was tactful and pragmatic. The children respected him and his authority. He was kind, yet firm, and knew how to talk to the teenagers. We told them that they had the right to demand to go for military training, as the liberation struggle respected the rights of both men and women, young and old. However, we had a duty and responsibility to protect the lives of everyone in the camp under our care. It was a priority for all of us to set our country free, like other independent countries of the world – including our host country, Zambia. I told them, 'The struggle needs all the young people to join hands and to fight for our democratic rights and freedom. If it is not your turn at this moment to go to the war and fight, there is no need to rush because, believe me, your turn will come.' I told them to think long and hard because the war was getting more and more complicated due to modern military technology, which required SWAPO to have educated combatants who could operate and apply sophisticated military technologies.

The PLAN combatants took good care of us during the time we were in the forest. They cooked very early every morning and brought us warm meals in the forest once a day. We had to ration this food well so that it could last the whole day – breakfast, lunch and dinner. When the situation worsened, even the Zambian population who lived around Nyango camp were forced to abandon their homes and flee with us into the forest. They stayed with us only temporarily, then went to live with their relatives in villages that were not affected by the war.

5

ANGOLA

In 1980, I received a verbal message from our camp commander at Nyango that I should pack all my belongings and wait for the transport that would take me to Lusaka, from where I was booked to fly to Angola. I was told that there was an urgent message from the SWAPO headquarters that I was urgently needed in Angola. While I packed my belongings, I saw my toddlers shedding tears. I asked them what the matter was. 'We too want to go with Mukwahepo to Angola,' came the reply. I had not discussed my journey with my children. They might have heard me talking about it with another adult. But then I realised how important it was that I discuss it with them because they seemed to understand the impact my going away would have on their lives. So, I gathered all of them and explained my forthcoming journey to Angola. I had plenty of time while I waited for the transport, so I explained slowly. I answered all their questions until they understood.

I understood to some extent what these children were going through because I also felt sad to be parting with them. I had given them my best during the time I had been with them, but now that my service was needed more urgently at another SWAPO camp, the children and I needed to accept this as part of the nature of our struggle. We also had to trust that the SWAPO leadership would not leave them on their own, and that another suitable person would be appointed to take care of them. It was normal practice for the leadership to ensure that whoever took over my house would also take over the guardianship of these children. I was prepared to negotiate with SWAPO, however, for an extra ticket to take along with me the child who was given to me on the first day of her life. I felt that this child needed someone who understood her situation. Her mother had come to live with me when she was discharged from the hospital in Lusaka, but she never recovered enough to take on her motherly responsibilities.

It was not until my departure for Angola that I realised how much I meant to my people at Nyango camp. Some young mothers panicked because they thought they would lose their connection with me. Many of them made me feel connected to them beyond comradeship. News about my transfer spread from mouth to ear. One young mother, upon hearing that I was being called to Luanda, brought her baby girl to me, saying: 'Please, take my daughter with you wherever you are going.' The same thing happened with two other young comrades. I realised that I could not accept one child and reject the others. What explanation would I have for doing this? And if I rejected the children, what consequences would that have for their trust in me, or any other adult in the camp? Also, would there be place on the aeroplane to take any children along?

I explained to my comrades that, although I would love to take all their babies with me to Angola, I could not accept any child at that point because I was not yet fully briefed as to where exactly in Angola I was going and what I was going to do. Firstly, I might be sent to the war zone, where the safety of the children would be compromised. Secondly, I was not yet sure how many seats would be allocated to me on the flight. I was therefore reluctant to take any child along to Angola because, due to lack of space on the flight, I may end up having to leave that child in Lusaka.

Nevertheless, I inquired from the Nyango authorities about the possibility of taking the four children who were directly under my care along with me. After some conflicting information, I finally received a message to say that places for my four children had been secured, and that I could go with all of them. In Lusaka, I was given another child with whom I was to travel to Angola. I was told that when I arrived in Angola, I was to hand over this child to another comrade who was living in Luanda.

On arrival in Luanda, I was taken to a SWAPO house where Dr Theophilus Hingashikuka Hamutumbangela lived. Dr Hamutumbangela was a medical doctor who took care of people who had been physically injured and/or disabled by the war. He introduced me to the comrades. Some had been shot in the head, some had broken limbs, others had a leg or an arm missing. I was not psychologically prepared to see my comrades disfigured in this manner, despite knowing that war kills, injures and maims people. I found it extremely difficult to work with these war victims. It broke my heart every time I looked at them, and I had to fight back my tears. What helped me to get used to them was their sense of humour and their high morale. Some of them had had their legs blown off by landmines; others had been injured in battle, having been shot in the eye or arm. Still others had their whole chest or a limb in plaster of Paris. We had to take care of them in almost every respect – cook for them, feed them (or at least those who did not have arms), and wash them (or assist them to wash themselves). After about two months, a message came from SWAPO headquarters for me to go to Kwanza-Sul to join *Meme* Lydia Ndadi and *Meekulu* Tresina Mukwaanime Nghimwena, to take care of SWAPO's children.

******

Kwanza-Sul was another one of SWAPO's settlements for its civilian population. It had been founded to accommodate the women and children who had been displaced by the devastating SADF attack on Cassinga on 4 May 1978. After the Cassinga massacre, it was not feasible for the survivors to continue living in the temporary evacuation tents that had been erected. It was felt that keeping the survivors within the vicinity of their ruined camp, and subjecting them to its presence, would be counter to their healing process. The hope was to evacuate the survivors and move them far away from Cassinga. Many were evacuated to Yamba[39] and Lubango, and finally to Kwanza-Sul.

The government of the People's Republic of Angola provided immense humanitarian support by evacuating the wounded to various Angolan hospitals, transporting the survivors by road to safer areas, collecting the bodies of the dead, and providing logistical support, food and medicine. It also generously made an area available in the Kwanza-Sul Province, to where the survivors were evacuated. Thereafter, the place became generally known as Kwanza-Sul. This support was given without the expectation of anything in return. The government of

---

39 Yamba was another SWAPO camp for women and young children that was situated about 60 km from Cassinga.

the Republic of Cuba also gave its support by taking several hundred children survivors and placing them in school in Cuba.

The logistical challenges were enormous, such as attending to the sick, cooking and distributing food, supplying blankets and tents to everyone, and helping the children to recover from the trauma. In the end, SWAPO divided up the people into different camps within Kwanza-Sul, so that there was a camp for the injured, for mothers, for kindergarten children, for school-going children, and for administration. This helped to direct expertise to support specific needs and for the survivors to support one another within their areas of need. We were brought to Kwanza-Sul to provide motherly support to the children who had survived the massacre. Many of these children had been orphaned by the attack. We were brought in to take care of children between the ages of two and ten years old. As senior adults in the camp, we also provided support and advice to the teenagers at the Namibia Education Centre.

On arrival at Kwanza-Sul, I was warmly received by the camp authorities and taken straight to my duty station, the Namibia Education Centre. Here I found *Meekulu* Tresina Mukwaanime Nghimwena, affectionately known as Mukwaanime waNghimwena, waiting for me. It was evidently clear that I had been expected. A room had been prepared for me and I was well briefed about my duties with the children. Comrade Nangolo Mbumba, one of our young comrades whom SWAPO had sent to study in the USA, was the school principal. He was an educated man but did not treat me as his inferior. Rather, he welcomed me in a highly respectful manner and spoke to me as if I were a very important person. I was truly moved by the manners of this young, tall, slender man, who briefed me in full the following morning. He was very earnest, and seriously committed to ensuring the recovery of the children. I promised to do my very best.

******

Dr Iyambo Indongo, whom I have introduced earlier, and his family were living at Cabuta in Kwanza-Sul when I arrived. He was greatly respected by the comrades there, who told me that he had been there since the establishment of Kwanza-Sul in 1978. I was told that Dr

Indongo was living at Yamba at the time of the Cassinga massacre. On that day, he and his family had seen the SADF bomber planes circling Cassinga and dropping the bombs on the camp. The thunderous sound could be heard as far afield as Yamba. Dr Indongo and his driver, Juuso, bravely drove the ambulance from Yamba to go and rescue people. They were spotted by the enemy bomber pilots, who dropped bombs on them too. Although the ambulance was damaged, this did not deter them from continuing their journey. They skillfully drove until they reached Cassinga. Dr Indongo is well respected for his commitment at having lived and survived with his people through the most difficult times.

Dr Indongo was known as the 'Bush Doctor'. I never asked why he had been given this name, and am not sure whether he himself was aware of it. When one of the children under my care became ill, some comrades advised me to take the child to the 'Bush Doctor' at Cabuta, because he would make him well. Dr Indongo is a humble man of very few words, a soft-spoken and kind gentleman. The nurses at Kwanza-Sul spoke of him with great respect, while his patients demanded his services without end. Dr Indongo, as well as Dr Amathila, was a very dedicated doctor who served his patients with dedication during the long and bitter struggle.

******

When we arrived at Kwanza-Sul, we found the camp full of children. There were about six hundred children between the ages of three and nine in the Education Centre. Although some children had their mothers living in other camps within Kwanza-Sul, they had come to live at the Education Centre so that they could easily go to kindergarten or school. Some children did not know where their mothers were. It was easier to trace the parents of the children who came from Yamba because there was a register of birth records. However, the majority of the children at Kwanza-Sul came from Cassinga, and there was not one single record about them because the documents had burnt during the bombing. They were just children of SWAPO in the SWAPO camps.

We found some of the children in a very poor condition and realised that we had to help them to improve their situation. Many of them had not had the opportunity to learn appropriate and acceptable behaviour. Also, they did not wash themselves properly or regularly, and did not wear clean clothes. Their hygiene was a cause for concern. So, we started calling meetings with the children, aimed at having conversations with them about their lives. We had to show them that they were significant and valuable; that their stories were important and interesting. As they spoke, we asked them to sit on our laps. We sat with them at their level – not on chairs while they sat on the floor. We all sat on the floor and talked as a group of equals. We did this until they realised that we were their friends.

We also saw that many of the children did not wear shoes. We wanted to know why, because every child in exile received shoes and clothes. Every caretaker of children went at least three times a year to the SWAPO store to select shoes and clothes for the children. There was enough clothing in the SWAPO camps for every person. SWAPO received a lot of quality clothes from Sweden, Finland, Denmark and Norway, the Swedes being especially supportive in the donation of children's clothes. It therefore did not make any sense to us that these children went barefoot.

We also noticed that some of the children had difficulty walking. '*Ounona otava tengenya va yuka kufye tava honyaeke*' – we called them to us, one by one, to sit on our laps or next to us. The children limped towards us. We examined them and saw that their feet and toes were rotting! They had septic sores that covered their feet (and in some cases their fingers too), caused by sand fleas (*oitakaya*). We had heard a great deal about the sand fleas of Kwanza-Sul. These parasitical insects live in the soil but can get inside your skin if you come into direct contact with the soil, for instance by walking barefoot, or through your fingers, and particularly under your fingernails. Once inside your body, they multiply very quickly and can cause serious infection. We therefore called the boys and girls to us individually to examine their feet, hands and hair. We were shocked to see how many of the children had been infected in this way. Their toes had become breeding grounds for these sand fleas and were almost eaten up completely. What remained were septic wounds covering their toe bones. This was causing them absolute misery.

We solicited information and opinions from the nurses and other adults at Kwanza-Sul regarding how these children had become so badly infected and how we could help them to recover. We were advised to carefully remove the insects from the children's feet using sterile needles.

First, we collected soap, towels, salt, Vaseline, buckets, water storage containers and washbasins from the stores. All of this was supplied to us free of charge. Then we asked some of the children who could still walk properly to go and collect water from the water points and firewood from the camp's main kitchen. As soon as the water and firewood was secured, we started boiling the water in large pots. While the water was on the fire, we started removing the sand fleas carefully from the children's feet and fingernails. This was a long and painful process because we had to be very careful not to prick the fleas, which would then release their eggs into the child's body to continue their life cycle. As we removed the sand fleas one by one, the children cried and screamed from the pain. It was an irritatingly painful process for us too, but this was the only way to do it. We then washed each child's feet and hands and soaked them in lukewarm salt water, which was our disinfectant. Finally, we rubbed Vaseline into their skin, to protect it and make it soft. At the same time, we taught the children about general hygiene and cleanliness. We told them to wash their bodies every night before going to bed, especially their feet, so that the sand fleas would not penetrate their flesh again.

There were many children and it took us more than a month of carefully removing sand fleas one by one, child by child, then washing them properly. In some cases, we had to teach them how to wash their bodies with soap and to comb their hair. We then showed the children where and how to collect water from the water points by going with them and doing it together. We taught them how to queue in an orderly manner with the rest of the camp residents to wait their turn to get water. We had large, five-hundred litre containers in which we stored water for cooking, drinking and washing, and had to make several trips to the water points to collect enough water to fill them.

With the help of some of the teachers in the camp, we started building washing shelters with sticks and bushes. We worked really hard, and in a matter of hours we had completed separate shelters for boys and girls. The children were great and they also worked hard, although there were a handful who refused to cooperate, especially in the beginning. We boiled water in our large pots. From then on, starting at four o'clock every afternoon, each child would take a washbasin of warm water into the washing shelter and wash.

Lice were another hygiene problem at the camp. The lice laid their eggs in the warmth of the children's hair. The easiest solution was to shave off all the hair of the infected children and then wash them thoroughly. We showed them how to apply Vaseline to their clean bodies and rub it in nicely until their skin was smooth and shiny. Every single evening we had to make sure that the children washed before supper and, above all, washed their feet before going to bed. If their feet were clean, there would be no chance for sand fleas to penetrate their skin.

It was hard work teaching the children personal hygiene, but it was gratifying and we were encouraged because they made positive progress in a very short period of time. A great number of them learnt how to take care of themselves independently, and maintained the discipline required to wash every evening before going to bed. What was most encouraging was that the children learnt not only from us but from each other. When they saw other children wearing shoes and clean clothes, they did the same, although they were only able to wear shoes once their feet had healed. We took all the children to the SWAPO store, which we called 'The Magazine', to select shoes and clothes.

We were amazed at the children's appreciation of beauty and neatness. They proudly washed their bodies and applied Vaseline until they shone. They combed and plaited their hair, and put on clean clothes. They learnt how to respond to the changes in their natural environment and to dress appropriately when it was cold, when it was raining, or when it was hot. As soon as we had established that the children had learnt to take care of themselves, we stopped interfering in their washing and dressing. All we monitored was that they were collecting water for washing every day. We continued to check their physical appearance to ensure that they looked clean, were dressed in clean clothes, and wore proper shoes on their feet.

Once the question of hygiene was sorted out, we turned our full attention to the children's food and nutrition. We put them on a strict eating plan of three meals a day. Although this plan was already in place before we came to Kwanza-Sul, many of the children did not bother to pay any attention to it. We decided to enforce it as part of our responsibility to ensure that the children ate well both before and after they went to kindergarten or school, and that they remained healthy and looked neat and beautiful. Once the children had eaten, their time was their own. They could play and get as dirty as they liked, as long as they washed again in the evening and maintained a high hygienic standard, which was required to stay healthy – indeed to survive – in the harsh natural environment of Kwanza-Sul. We also inspected them in the evenings, to make sure that they slept in their rooms and on their beds. This was tough work that required our complete commitment. It is no joke to work with children.

******

Whilst the development of the majority of the children went smoothly, there were a few cases of stubborn ones who would not listen to any of our advice. They did not want to follow any instructions or guidance from us because prior to our arrival they were the ones giving the orders. Our presence took away their power. They ordered the other children around and bullied them. At first we were surprised when some of the children left their food untouched and went to eat unripe dates, mealies, guavas, bananas and palm fruits. These children would go onto the Angolan subsistence farms to secretly steal these fruit and vegetables while the other children were at school. We did not understand this because we had enough food in the camp. When we took the children to the SWAPO store to get shoes and clothes, certain children selected clothes that were much too big for them. They folded the bottoms of their oversized trousers and tied them with a rope so that they fitted in the waist. We simply could not understand their behaviour.

Meme Lydia Ndadi had a strong character and did not give up. Even with the most stubborn cases and when the situation seemed hopeless, she continued to advise and talk to these children. She encouraged us to proactively engage the children, saying that we should try to understand them and their behaviour. If we did not understand the reasons for their attitude, the thing that had triggered this behaviour may continue, and the situation could get worse. 'Children are children,' she said. 'They need us, all of them need a mother, and we are their mothers. War has exposed these children to many things, which even they may have difficulty explaining. Most of these children came from the Cassinga camp that was bombed by the enemy two years ago. Some of these behaviours may be triggered by the effect of the war, or they may be a reaction to missed opportunities, such as having a normal family life with a mum and a dad. It could be that they are reacting to or rebelling against something. Or they are going through the phase of puberty, and are testing their will against ours. So, being their friends is the best thing we can do. We need to show them that we are here to serve them and their needs.'

While she advised us about how to get on with the children, she also spoke to the children calmly, in a way that made them think further than their immediate needs. I can recall one day when she spoke to a group of young boys between the ages of seven and twelve. She told them, 'We are Namibians, hosted by the Angolan government and people, who have accepted us into their country out of solidarity and support for our independence struggle. The Angolan government has allocated us land on which to stay. We live here at Kwanza-Sul because the residents of this area accepted and welcomed us. We were not put here to destroy the agricultural produce and the livelihood of the Angolans in their own country. Therefore, you must behave yourselves and respect the Angolan citizens and their property. They have given us shelter in their own country, in the spirit of solidarity and comradeship. We should not return their kindness with disrespect and abuse. If you continue stealing and destroying the property of our host, one day they may get angry and chase us away from this place, and from their country. Can any of you tell me what country we would go to if we were chased away from Angola? Do you know of any country that would accept people with unruly behaviour? Think about all the people in this camp. What would happen to them if we were kicked out of Kwanza-Sul? We must therefore behave respectfully towards the Angolans and their property. We cannot return their kindness with reckless behaviour.'

The children listened, and many of them stopped stealing the farm produce. Then we realised that every morning after breakfast, some of the children were going back to their rooms. Later, when the other children went to kindergarten or school, they roamed around the camp. So, not only did we have to ensure that the children received their porridge on time in the mornings to enable them to go to school, but also that they actually got to classes. Every morning at quarter to eight, one of us would go from room to room, checking to see who went back to sleep after breakfast, and why. In a few cases, the children used sickness as an excuse for not going to school after breakfast. But most of the stubborn ones told us to our faces that they did not want to go to school.

We sometimes found sick children in the rooms who had not been reported to us as being unwell by the other children. We later discovered that the children were afraid to tell us that these children had not come to breakfast or had failed to go to school because a child who told on others was stigmatised, and called a 'taleteller'. No child wanted this label. We had to explain to them that it was normal for children and adults to get sick, and that when a child was sick, the children who are well must report the sick child to us. We would then take the sick child to the hospital, where the doctor and nurses would make that child well again. We had to explain to the children that this was part of our work. We had not come to Kwanza-Sul to punish children. We had come to take care of them because we loved them, like the grandmothers do back home.

We routinely checked the children's rooms every morning for sick children, or for those avoiding going to school. We took the sick ones to the hospital, and made sure they took their medicine, ate well and rested. We also spoke to their roommates, asking them to take care of them while they were sick. It was important that the children learnt the basic skill of taking care of others. We told them that they were helping us by reporting all the sick children, and taking food to them. We were the ones who ensured that the sick children took their medicine. Children who were too sick to live with the others were brought to live with us until they were well enough to return to their rooms. The system worked well, and the children started taking care of themselves and taking on the responsibility of caring for others and reporting to us when they needed help. We spoke on a regular basis to the children who refused to go to school until they got used to us and realised that we were not out to punish them, but rather to try and teach them the basic skills they would need in life. Eventually, they came around, and started going to school like all the other children.

******

In 1987, the SWAPO office at Kwanza-Sul informed me that I was wanted in Luanda, so I quickly packed my few belongings and left for Luanda. Here I was given a plane ticket to Lubango, whereupon my arrival I was told that I was to receive into my care a baby girl whose mother was too ill to take care of her. The SWAPO leadership had decided that I should take the child and look after her. That was it. I got the baby. I spoke to the mother and then went back to Kwanza-Sul with her.

A year later, the child passed away whilst under my care. This was so bad. It broke my heart. Why should a baby die under my care, and in my hands? The death of this baby made me realise how complicated it was to raise a child who was not biologically or legally my own. The death of this child made me think so many thoughts. One of them was that her biological mother was far away in Lubango, and I had no means of informing her about the severity of her child's sickness while she was still alive. The child's mother only found out about the death of her baby when she was already dead and buried. We had to bury her in the absence of her mother because we had no facilities at Kwanza-Sul to keep her body for a long period of time. Oh, I had never experienced a thing like this in my whole life.

Thank God, the mother came about a month after the burial. She had a strong character and was very calm, peaceful and collected. I informed her about how her daughter had suddenly become ill. The child had received medical help as soon as we noticed that she was ill, but the treatment could not cure the illness. We all tried, but nothing helped. The mother accepted everything. But I just could not understand why God had taken this child away from me. Why?

The other thing was that the party leadership and the mother had entrusted this child to my care, and she had died in my hands, under my care. I still cannot understand this. I cannot. The image of this child has not left me. Every time I think of her – and several other comrades dearest to us who died in exile – it makes me sad. I realise that their remains have been left behind, and we cannot even go there to clean their graves or bring flowers to them at their resting places. We welcome peace in Angola and hope it will enable us to visit our deceased comrades, our children that we had to leave behind in their final resting places, especially in Angola and Zambia.

******

There were many teenage girls and boys at Kwanza-Sul, as well as young adults who had come from Namibia to join the liberation struggle. As an adult and a woman, I was concerned about the wellbeing of our girls between the ages of thirteen and nineteen; about how they were socialising amongst themselves and with visitors, especially men who were much older and more experienced than themselves. You must understand that even during war, human beings never stop being human. They do things and react and respond to each other the same way, even during difficult times. We felt that since we were the elders in the camp, we were the mothers of these girls and should talk to them about their lives, their futures and their education. We therefore organised meetings with them. We advised them about the importance of education, and encouraged them to take seriously the education they were receiving at Kwanza-Sul. We explained the opportunities that SWAPO was giving to young people who had an active interest in pursuing their educational goals.

We also advised them to take care of themselves well and to resist the temptation of getting into sexual relationships. We said they should try to behave in the same manner as they would if they were in Namibia with their parents. We encouraged the older girls to look after the younger ones. These teenage girls were the nicest group of people to talk to. They agreed with everything we said, were polite and well mannered. They never answered back. They were unlike our children born in exile, who asked questions and demanded explanations. These girls listened carefully and agreed with everything. We thought – how understanding, how responsible! We returned to our side of the camp feeling very gratified.

However, as things turned out, we had totally misunderstood these teenagers. Although when we had talked to them they had humbly listened to every word we had said with utmost respect, suddenly they began falling pregnant, one after another. We were shocked because when we had spoken to them about sexual relationships, they had responded very responsibly and innocently. We had told them that although earthly pleasures may end, education – once you have it – is yours forever. We encouraged the boys regarding education too. They often argued with us that they wanted to go to the front, not stay in the camps like women and children. But we told them that even if they wanted to join the armed struggle, SWAPO needed educated soldiers to operate big guns, which required a good knowledge of mathematics and physical science. We told them that they were fortunate to have gone into exile at a young age because SWAPO was actively looking out for opportunities to send young people to school. We did not want them to miss out on these opportunities. I had seen in Tanzania that newly independent countries needed educated people to run them. The job of all young people in SWAPO was to study. We advised them to study, and study hard, so that when they returned to Namibia after independence they would be able to uplift their communities out of poverty.

Our talk had obviously not achieved what we thought it had and the teenage girls continued to fall pregnant. The next time we talked to them we were met with silence. This was a wake-up call and, as a carer of children, I was not only shocked but embarrassed. Yet we continued to talk to the girls, including those who had fallen pregnant, about not giving up on their education. We could not give up on them because we were their mothers and grandmothers. We were not against pregnancy. We were doing our job as parents to regulate the behaviour of our young people. We truly wanted them to complete grade 12 so that they would have possibilities open to them in the future. Further talks with the teenage girls revealed that while some of them had fallen pregnant after arriving at Kwanza-Sul, several had done so during their journey into exile. Some of these relationships had been with boyfriends with whom they had travelled from home; others had been with the SWAPO combatants who had escorted them during their journey to Kwanza-Sul.

Some of the male teachers at Kwanza-Sul contributed to the high rate of pregnancy amongst the teenage girls. It was forbidden within SWAPO for teachers to take advantage of their position by having relationships with their pupils. Despite this, some teachers targeted these girls as objects of their pleasure. Then, when one of them fell pregnant, the teacher would warn her not to expose him. The teachers feared they would be reassigned if SWAPO found out that they had abused their positions. Teachers who had relationships with their pupils were immediately transferred to other duties where they would not endanger young people. Apparently, once a teacher discovered that a girl was pregnant, he would threaten her, saying that if she informed the administration that he was responsible for her pregnancy, he would dump her immediately and would not give any support to her or to her unborn baby. Most of the teachers at Kwanza-Sul were married. As would be the case in most societies, the male teachers were afraid of the consequences for their marriage if their wives found out that they had made a pupil pregnant. This was another reason for a teacher exerting pressure on a pregnant girl not to reveal him. Naïvely, the young girls covered up for the teachers out of fear of losing their support. They would give their babies false names, such as Bazooka, to try to cover up the identity of the father. But, as the truth always comes out, so the name of the father would eventually come out.

Once we realised what was happening, we started visiting the teenagers' dormitories in the evenings to check that they were in their beds. We wanted them to realise that they were not living in a place of disorder, and that we expected them to behave in an acceptable manner.

The teenagers were very clever and were always thinking ahead of us. When they realised that we were checking up on them, they devised a plan. They would make their beds nicely and roll up a blanket, which they would put under the bedding to resemble the body of a sleeping person covered from head to toe, so that when we went into their dormitories, we would think they were in their beds, asleep, and leave without disturbing them. One day, we decided to check. We lifted the bedding and, to our shock, found the rolled-up blankets in their beds instead of them. The rooms were empty. The girls were gone.

What else could we do? We just continued talking to them. Some of them took our advice more seriously, especially after learning lessons from their peers who had fallen pregnant. Unfortunately, some ended up learning the hard way. We used to tell them, 'If you miss out on the opportunity to go to school while you are in exile, what will you take home to Namibia after independence? What will you bring to your parents? Do you want to return home with nothing but poverty? You were poor when you left Namibia, and it would be a great pity if you returned home to your parents with that same poverty, despite the fact that here in exile SWAPO gave you the opportunity to further your education. You came into exile to make a difference. Why throw away your future, your education?'

I was really worried. It pained me to see these girls falling pregnant. I suffered a blow when it happened to one girl whom I really liked because of her outstanding achievement at school. I cried the day she left the Education Centre for the mothers' camp. Even today, when I think of it, I feel sad. I am not against pregnancy – I love children, and think they have the right to life. What I am against is children becoming sexually active at a very early age and becoming involved in sexual relationships without understanding the consequences. In some cases, these girls did not know who the father of their child was. That was a great pity because many combatants felt honoured to have someone carrying their babies. Some of the young mothers became unhappy throughout their pregnancies. They also suffered postnatal trauma. It was only when they were confronted with the consequences of their behaviour that they realised that their opportunity to go to school and study, as all children ought to do, had been ruined.

SWAPO actively solicited educational support for its young people to go and study abroad. Many of our young girls and boys received scholarships to go and finish their secondary schooling in West Africa. These countries, such as Cameroon, Sierra Leone, Ghana, Nigeria, The Gambia and Senegal, contributed immensely by educating young Namibians in their countries. Also, a SWAPO kindergarten was opened in N'dalatando in Angola, which took quite a number of children from Kwanza-Sul. Another SWAPO Education Centre was opened in Loudima in the south of Congo-Brazzaville, where hundreds of our teenage children went for schooling. SWAPO children in exile were also generously schooled overseas, in countries with which we had friendly relations, such as Cuba, the German Democratic Republic (GDR) and Czechoslovakia. This support was greatly appreciated, especially as our student population at Kwanza-Sul kept on growing, as new babies were being born and more young Namibians were joining SWAPO from Namibia.

Kwanza-Sul was an interesting place to live. It had a life of its own and, even though we were in a war situation, people were happy. Everyone was kind and helpful towards each another. An individual struggle was a shared struggle. We tried to create a real family life within the camp. Just as we would have done had we been in Namibia, we celebrated the birth, name-giving and baptism of our newborn babies, as well as the weddings of those who entered into matrimonial unions. Our parties in exile were really fun, even when there was not that much to offer those attending the ceremonies. People shared whatever they had. I often took care of the personal belongings of comrades moving to other SWAPO camps, or going to school. Comrade Rosalia left me with her suitcase in which her beautiful wedding dress was packed. This dress was borrowed time and again by several people who got married at Kwanza-Sul and who did not have a wedding dress of their own. Rosalia lent it out generously. Couples used it responsibly and returned it without a mark on it. The spirit of Kwanza-Sul is something not easily found elsewhere. I do not know any woman that easily and generously lends her wedding dress to anyone who asks for it. In Kwanza-Sul, this generosity was a way of life.

Every joyful event was a reason to celebrate. As it was wartime and the enemy never sleeps, we celebrated responsibly. If someone named a child after you, it was a reason to celebrate; to remember and be remembered. Our celebrations were orderly. Nonsense behaviour was not tolerated. People looked after themselves well. They dressed smartly every day. Everything we did was done to perfection. With very few ingredients, we prepared wonderful meals and enjoyed them as a group. Fish was delivered to us monthly, or even sometimes weekly. It was a large part of our diet as well as our social life in the camp. We went as individuals and in groups to collect the fish and dry it. We cooked it fresh and dried. Thinking about it, I had more food in the SWAPO camps than I ever had again in my life. SWAPO had mobilised great support from international and multilateral organisations, as well as from friendly governments. It was mainly due to this solidarity, generosity and support that we could maintain a social life in the camps.

Shikongo shaHangala came to Kwanza-Sul to get married while I was there. He had found someone with whom to share his life. I attended his wedding and was glad to see him looking truly happy and handsome on his wedding day. He deserved to be happy. He was a wonderful man with a beautiful personality. I was very glad that fate had brought him to Kwanza-Sul so that I could witness his wedding. I too had my fair share of dreams, but none of them came true. And, considering the life that I lived in exile, always surrounded by the children, what time would I have had to invest in a relationship? I accept my life as it is. I want to believe that each one of us has a purpose in life, and that I served mine.

6

THE COMING OF INDEPENDENCE

We received the news about the implementation of UN Resolution 435 in June of 1989. We were at Kwanza-Sul, going about our business as usual, when suddenly there was an urgent call from the camp commander for all residents to speedily gather at the parade. When we arrived there, we saw that we had visitors. The camp commander called the parade to order and immediately introduced Comrade Nekongo, the first camp commander of Kwanza-Sul, who had just arrived from the SWAPO headquarters in Luanda. Comrade Nekongo in turn introduced the visiting SWAPO delegation. He told us that the purpose of their mission was to bring the delegation from the United Nations to Kwanza-Sul. He said that they had to deliver a very important message in the presence of the UN delegates, and that we should listen well. He said that if we needed clarity, we should feel free to ask questions openly.

The official from SWAPO headquarters told us that the negotiations at the United Nations regarding the implementation of UN Resolution 435 had been successful. The UN member countries, including those with veto powers, had all voted in favour of the implementation of Resolution 435. This meant the beginning of the peaceful transition to independence for Namibia.

He told us that the South African government had also agreed to the implementation of the UN resolution. SWAPO had made its commitment and had fully endorsed the UN decision. He said, 'You must therefore all return to your rooms and start packing your belongings because you are going home. SWAPO is going home to prepare its political campaign for the planned independence election. Amongst other things, UN Resolution 435 stipulates that a free and fair election must be held in Namibia to determine the political party that is going to rule the country after independence. We will have to prepare an election campaign to explain to the Namibian people why they should vote for us, what development programmes we have for the country, and what we would do for the country if we were to take over the government. There are several procedures we will have to follow.'

We were also told that on our arrival in Namibia, we should return to our homes, our villages, our towns from where we originally came. We were told that when we arrived home we should integrate ourselves back into society; that we should not isolate ourselves from our brothers and sisters.

They explained to us that repatriation was voluntary; that no one was being forced into it. We were informed that, firstly, each Namibian resident of Kwanza-Sul who chose to be repatriated was to be photographed and issued with an identity document. This would be the person's passport to get to Namibia. We were to carry this travel document at all times so that we could be identified throughout our journey from Angola to Namibia. The UN delegates who had accompanied the SWAPO officials were responsible for this registration process, and they wanted to start as soon as the meeting had ended. The UN officials did not say anything during the meeting. They merely observed, and listened to what the SWAPO official was saying to us. They waited patiently for the meeting to end to see whether people would come forward to be registered for the voluntary repatriation to Namibia.

This news, although positive and long awaited, seemed too good to be true. It came as a shock, even though we had awaited it for years and years. It was too sudden. The people were so stunned that when Comrade Nekongo asked whether there were any questions, or if anything needed clarification, the whole parade was silent. Not a single question was asked. There was nothing to say. The delegation from Luanda then started with the registration process.

They asked the people who were ready to be repatriated to line up so they could be photographed. One by one we were photographed. The person who took our photographs gave each of us a number. We then moved to the next queue, where we presented our number and were registered. The registration officers asked us for a lot of information, which they wrote onto a very long form. Amongst other things, they asked for our name, surname, date of birth, place of birth, the year we had joined SWAPO, the year we had gone into exile. They asked whether or not we wanted to be repatriated voluntarily. There were just too many questions popping into our heads. Yet, despite all these questions and the anxiety we felt, the process of voluntary registration went on until every man, woman and child in the camp was registered. Not one single person refused to be repatriated. At some stage I became worried. I wondered whether these people were serious. What if this was a trick to take us to Namibia and sell us to the enemy?

So, we queued voluntarily and were registered. The UN officials were registering people for as long as there was light to see what they were writing. We had to fill in the forms in triplicate, with three photographs per person. One set of papers went to the UN, the second to SWAPO headquarters, and the third was returned to us with our ID document. Finally, we were asked to go to the clinic for a vaccination, after which we had to present the vaccination card we had been given to the registration officer so it could be noted on our form.

As I have said, all this information was processed into SWAPO ID cards that were our travel documents for our journey from Kwanza-Sul to Namibia, via Luanda and Lubango. A person without this ID document would not be able to board a flight or be transported by any kind of vehicle to Namibia. The ID card was therefore a crucial document.

SWAPO used the information on our forms to organise transport for us to get to Namibia. Each of us had to stipulate on our registration form where we wanted to be repatriated to. There were different officials designated to help people heading to each particular destination. If you stated that you wished to be repatriated to Windhoek, then the officials responsible for placing people on flights going to Windhoek would handle your repatriation and arrange for you to be put on a flight to that destination. We were asked to think carefully before indicating where we wanted to go. Some people indicated that they wanted to go to Oshakati, and later found out that all their friends were going to Windhoek. But they could not just swop places with someone. They had to alter their destination officially and then follow another process to be reallocated transport to their changed destination.

I registered myself, together with all the children under my direct care who had not been claimed by their biological parents. A great number of parents came to collect their children from me while I was still at Kwanza-Sul. SWAPO had encouraged us to travel home with our families, and made it possible for people to collect their children from any SWAPO camp in Angola or Zambia. They could then register their children themselves, and all travel home together as a family. Although I expected all the parents of my children to collect them from me, this did not happen. I had six children who were not collected, so I registered them to be repatriated with me as my family, and happily travelled with them to Namibia.

While in exile, we had to try hard to suppress thoughts and feelings about home to avoid becoming homesick. At times I had doubted whether I would live to see Namibia again. Perhaps it would only be the younger generation who would see our independence, while we, the old ones, would only be history. When I thought of the many comrades with whom I had been in the liberation struggle, several of whom had sacrificed their lives for it, I could not help wondering how many of us would live to see the independence of our country. These questions had come into my mind: Will I ever set foot in a free and independent Namibia? How many of us will be fortunate enough to do so?

At the parade we had been told that independence was coming; that we should pack all our belongings because the hour had come for us to go home. And this time it was for real. Who could believe this news; that we were indeed going home to our mothers, to our fathers, to our brothers and sisters? The war was over. Independence was coming. I was truly overjoyed – this was a real victory, a big victory for us. I arrived back at my house and sat on my bed, my mind went wild. So many thoughts ran through my head. I was thinking and hoping, but I was also doubting. I wondered whether this was true. Maybe it was just a strategy to give us false hope. Was I dreaming this, or did they really say that we were going home? My brain was swinging back and forth with all these thoughts. Other people were also experiencing similar thoughts and were talking to each other, trying to digest what they had just heard at the parade. By the time I came out of my reverie and looked outside, people were busy packing their belongings and preparing to return to Namibia. The joy of going home filled the air.

Yet, on that first day, after we had heard the news that we were going home, I could not pack a single thing. I just could not. All I could do was sit quietly in my house. I did not go anywhere or do anything. I just sat. When I think about it now, I know that my reaction to the news about our forthcoming independence was one of total shock. Independence was what we had wanted so badly that when our colonisers had refused to give it to us in a peaceful manner, we had decided to fight until we had won it. Throughout my twenty-four years in the struggle, every day and every night, I had waited for independence. And yet, when this news finally came, I was so shocked by it that I could not do a thing. I just wanted to be left alone to cry, hard and loud.

I recalled the time when we had started the South West Africa Liberation Army (SWALA).[40] Namibia, a country that hardly had a knobkerrie, had decided to fight a nation that had modern weapons and military equipment. Our combatants had engaged the enemy despite the many challenges. One of these was transport. Our guerrilla fighters had to walk long and arduous distances to do battle, carrying with them not only very heavy arms and ammunition, but also all their food and medicine. The South African soldiers, on the other hand, travelled in sophisticated military vehicles that were tailor-made for combat action. The enemy had personnel carriers and fighter-bomber military aircraft. Yet we had won our independence despite these huge odds. It had come about due to the selflessness and self-sacrifice of our PLAN fighters, who knew that the enemy had advanced weapons, and money to buy mercenaries from any country in the world, yet fought on regardless.

Perhaps you can understand my shock, therefore, when I finally heard the news that the war was over and we were on our way to independence. Had South Africa really surrendered? Had the enemy really given up the fight, or were they just using this ceasefire as a trick

---

40 Later renamed the People's Liberation Army of Namibia (PLAN).

to get us all home in order to cage us? What if we went home to Namibia, only to be handed over to the apartheid government as prisoners? I was not really sure what to expect regarding this news. We were just told over and over again about a UN decision. We did not really know who had brought us this message in the name of the UN. It was really tough on us to be told something so enormous, and then be expected to believe it on the spot.

My confusion was made worse by the fact that no one could reassure us that it was safe to go home. After the SWAPO and UN officials left, we had many questions for which we could get no answers. Although we had been well informed at the parade, and had been given the chance to ask questions, no one had done so. And although all the residents of the camp had heard the news for themselves, and were ululating with joy while they packed their belongings, a cloud of uncertainty was on the face of every adult in the camp.

Yet we knew that the UN envoy had been brought to Kwanza-Sul by SWAPO cadres. Comrade Nekongo was the first camp commander of Kwanza-Sul, and we trusted that SWAPO would only send him to our camp on a serious mission.

Eventually, things began to settle. My body and soul accepted the idea that we were going home and other thoughts started rolling into my mind. I began thinking about the specifics of going home. Would I find my mother alive? If not, where would I go? My father had died when I was a baby. What about my brother, Rafael, and my sister, Maria? If my mother was no longer alive, would I then go to live with my paternal uncle, the one who had taken care of me after my father's death? Or, if both my mother and paternal uncle had passed away, would I go and live with my brother?

I also thought that as I would be too old to work in an independent Namibia, I would perhaps be allocated a government house in which to live. I knew that the socialist governments in Eastern Europe had allocated government houses to elderly people who had served the party during difficult times. These people had workers to clean their homes, wash their clothes and cook for them. They were also provided with free medical services and other privileges from their government until they died. I therefore thought that, since SWAPO had been following the socialist model of development, if they won the election they would remember the SWAPO veterans, and I may be allocated a government house. During my stay in Tanzania, I had seen how the Tanganyika African National Union (TANU) veterans had lived in houses allocated to them by the party after independence. I therefore assumed that the same thing would happen with a SWAPO government.

******

After we had registered, we waited for long weeks in Kwanza-Sul for the transport that would carry us and all our belongings to Luanda, from where we would fly to Namibia. Then, one afternoon, truck after truck after truck arrived to collect us. The camp authorities had informed us in detail about how the repatriation process would take place, so we had already moved our luggage that was going as cargo to the office, where it was loaded onto the trucks bound for Luanda. All the camp residents had been given brand new bags in which to pack the belongings with which they would travel. The rest of their things would go as cargo from Kwanza-Sul to the specific destinations in Namibia that they had indicated on their registration forms. Everything was done in a very orderly manner. All the items were marked properly and loaded onto the trucks, until they were full to the brim. After loading, each person moved away to give space to the next comrade to load his or her things.

The truck drivers, some of them Angolan comrades, were very helpful and polite. I did not have to lift a finger. They checked my papers, labelled all my belongings, and loaded them gently onto the truck. I was impressed. When each truck was full, it moved away and the next one pulled up, and so on until all the cargo was loaded. The fully loaded trucks were covered with plastic, probably to protect our things from getting wet. Once our luggage had gone, we waited for the civilian convoy that would take us to Luanda in the early hours of the morning.

I recall that no one in the camp slept that night. People talked all night long. Not only were they excited about going home, there was also some anxiety about the process of the implementation of UN Resolution 435. People were wondering how committed South Africa was to this process. So, people were happy, but at the same time their minds were going from pillar to post with anxiety. At two o'clock in the morning, we started boarding the trucks, following a similar procedure as we had done with our belongings. When the camp authorities saw me, they said, '*Meekulu* Mukwahepo, come this way.' I therefore proceeded with my children.

At about four o'clock, everyone was on board and the trucks were ready to move. Suddenly, I heard my name being called, 'Mukwahepo, Mukwahepo.'

'*Ai*, what is it now?' I said, getting down from the truck.

I was told by the officers in charge to disembark from the convoy and offload my belongings so that I could stay behind with Comrade Kaino,[41] a young mother who seemed mentally disturbed. Apparently, she had been told to climb onto a truck for hours, but instead had started shouting. The comrades in the truck in which she was meant to travel had become frightened. They apparently feared that she might bite them and pass on her 'sickness' to them. They did not know how to deal with her and were reluctant to travel in the same truck as she was in. They had therefore disembarked. She, in turn, had become uncomfortable being amongst people who were scared of every move she made, so she continued shouting and talking to herself loudly. This had resulted in a huge commotion. The camp commander believed that only I could resolve the situation. So they told me to stay behind to take care of her.

I must tell you, I was really shocked at this because there were medical personnel amongst the people in this convoy, people who were trained to deal with this sort of situation. Yet it seemed that the camp commander believed that I, Mukwahepo, was the one to calm and cure all ills. They were prepared to let everyone proceed with their journey whilst I struggled with Kaino. And what would I do if she had really gone mad, when all the medical personnel had left? I had to think fast. I decided to myself that I would not offload my things and I would not be left behind. We would all go together, as planned. I knew Kaino very

---

[41] Not her real name.

well because I had looked after her and her child in the camp on various occasions.

I walked straight up to her and held her hands. 'Come with me, Kaino,' I said in a very soft voice. 'Join me in the truck so that we can travel home together.' She listened, then followed me without any arguments. She took her belongings and we got onto the last truck, where there was still space for two people. We sat down quietly like everyone else and travelled to Luanda smoothly. People were shocked into silence. That was how it came about that I abandoned the truck with my children and my belongings in order to accompany my comrade who needed my support throughout this journey. I travelled with her until we got to Luanda. I was not worried about my things because my children were there to take care of them, and the comrades who were on that truck understood my situation and would take care of the children and our belongings. So there was nothing for me to worry about.

I left with the last convoy. Although this had happened by accident, I was one of the last SWAPO people to leave Kwanza-Sul, the place where our people had dwelled since 1978 when they were evacuated from Cassinga. It was only at that moment, when I saw the camp commander actually closing the camp gate, that the reality hit me, and I felt deep inside me the beginning of a new era. I felt totally overwhelmed. I was suddenly so sad to look at Kwanza-Sul. Tears dropped from my eyes. I cannot say whether they were tears of joy or sorrow, or both. That was it.

As soon as all the trucks were outside the Kwanza-Sul gate, the camp commander gave instructions and the trucks started to move away slowly, towards Cabuta, and then to Luanda. It was the longest convoy in which I have ever travelled. The line of trucks was about ten kilometres long. We drove for nearly eleven hours, stopping only for fuel and to give everyone an opportunity to respond to the call of nature. We then continued with our journey. The trucks were not just driven in any direction the driver pleased. No, the journey was organised very carefully. When a truck was left behind, the convoy would wait until all the trucks were together so that the journey could proceed. We drove like this until we arrived at the transit camp in Luanda.

******

At the transit camp in Luanda, we joined other comrades who were also waiting to return to Namibia. This was where we stayed for about a month, waiting to be repatriated. Later on, more comrades from other SWAPO centres in Angola joined us. While we were in this camp, I met the father of one of my children. He was a PLAN combatant who had come from the war zone. He asked me to give him his child because he wanted to travel home with her to Namibia. This comrade was so proud of his daughter, and grateful for the chance of having met up with her. He was seeing her for the first time. I doubted whether a PLAN combatant who had been in a war situation for many years could actually look after a child. Yet this man was so determined to have his daughter with him, and over the following days he proved to be very responsible.

There were times when I felt so sorry for him. I tried to imagine how overwhelming the experience must have been for him, to meet his daughter for the first time when she was seven years old. She was born while he was at the war zone and he did not get an opportunity to come to Kwanza-Sul to see her. I happily gave him his daughter and he was thrilled. Giving children back to their biological parents was very difficult for me to do. After having brought them up for several years, these children became part of me. Losing them was like losing a very big part of who I was. It was an emotional experience for both of us. The child went with her dad and, after walking about two hundred metres, ran back, hugged me and held on to me for a long time, crying. I did not cry because this would have broken the spirit with which all children should be reunited with their biological parents. I do not know exactly how the child felt parting with me, but I could see that we were both scared of losing a part of one another. Nevertheless, I continued with my journey to Namibia with the five children who had not yet been claimed by their biological parents.

Whilst at the transit camp in Luanda, I observed that our people did not take too kindly to Kaino. She was isolated from the rest of the comrades, and this worried me. Kaino was perfectly fine when she was with people she knew and with whom she was comfortable; people who accepted her for who she was. Unfortunately, when she was with strangers she became upset, especially if they were behaving emotionally, for instance, if they were screaming and laughing. Then she felt uncomfortable and became confused. Mostly she just talked to herself, but sometimes she went crazy and someone had to hold her. She was alright when people showed her some kindness. She was such a lovely girl, even when she lost control. The moment she noticed my presence, she quietened down. I always greeted her and asked her to come home with me.

I was the mother of every motherless person and took care of Kaino in the camp, making sure she received food and information. I also went with her to collect water. We slept in the same room and she never hurt me or any of the children. What worried me was that I had registered to be repatriated to Ondangwa, while Kaino was registered to go to Windhoek. I realised that it would be best if she travelled with me to Namibia. I therefore asked the officials if it would be possible to change her destination. I shared my concerns with them. I told them I wanted to ensure that she would get to Namibia and would be delivered to her parents. The officials had seen how she was almost removed from the convoy at Kwanza-Sul. Without any argument, they changed her destination from Windhoek to Ondangwa and rebooked her onto the same transport as me. They understood that she would need my help on the journey home.

MUKWAHEPO

7
RETURNING HOME

I left the transit camp in Luanda in August 1989 and, together with my five children and Comrade Kaino, flew to Ondangwa via Lubango. On arrival at Ondangwa airport, we were greeted by a jubilant group of SWAPO supporters who had come to welcome us and to look out for their relatives who had gone into exile. Oh, I was extremely delighted to see our people, young and old, men and women, joyfully welcoming us back to our motherland. Some of the people had walked long distances from their homes and villages to Ondangwa airport just to welcome us home. We were told during the briefing we received at the airport that these people had stood for hours waiting for us, determined to give us a heroic welcome. And they did not just stand and gaze at us. No, they sang revolutionary SWAPO songs. Some of the songs I was familiar with; others I had not heard before. I realised then that singing was an art form that people used to show their solidarity and comradeship.

I was overjoyed at our peaceful return. This was a dream come true. The determination shown by our people who had bravely come to welcome us at the airport, in broad daylight and despite the presence of the apartheid military and police, made me feel strongly that, yes, indeed, independence was coming. We joyfully climbed onto the big trucks that were waiting to transport us from the Ondangwa airport to the Engela Reception Centre.

******

Whilst at Engela, I found out that my mother had passed away. I was also told that my uncle, Haimini yaHalweendo, who had brought me up, was also deceased, as was his wife, my aunt. This news was a blow to my spirit and tore apart my mental preparedness for this homecoming. I was shocked. I was told that their son, Viitu yaHaimini, now lived at their homestead. Although this was my only consolation, I did not know whether Viitu would take kindly to accepting responsibility for me and my children.

This was a big problem for me. I was seriously concerned about where I would be going. I felt bad about the deaths of my mother and my paternal uncle. I had looked forward to seeing my mother. I had strong yearnings to see her, to hug her and tell her how much I had missed her and longed for her. I wanted to tell her that I had returned from exile. But she was no more. I felt sad. As a returnee, I had to look forward and be hopeful. Yet the news of my mother's death devastated my spirit. I tried to stop thinking about my loss, but no matter how hard I tried to suppress the thoughts and feelings, they kept coming back. As the saying goes in my mother tongue, '*Omukulunhu ohali ohonde notwila.*' This means that an elder has to eat blood and pus. There was no time to lose. I had five children and Kaino, and I needed to make a plan. The staff at Engela helped me to send a message to Kaino's family. A week later, her relatives came to take her home. I was very happy to see that she came from a very warm and loving family.

Having delivered Kaino to her relatives, my conscience was clear and I could continue with my journey to the Odibo Reception Centre with my five children. Odibo is situated about forty-five kilometres northeast of Ondangwa. The reception centre there was the closest one to my home village, Onengali yaKaluvi. Although I was close to home, I decided that the best thing to do would be to stay on at the centre until our things arrived in Ondangwa from Luanda. Going home with five children and not even a blanket to sleep on would be expecting too much of the people who would have to put us up.

Our things eventually arrived at Ondangwa airport. I did not have a car to collect them and bring them to Odibo, and I did not know anyone who had a car. Luckily, the officials who had received us, as well as the leaders of our group, were very concerned about me. This may have been because of my advanced age. I was happy to see that the people at the reception centre were trying to make life easier for the old and the fragile. Every time the staff members heard of a car going to Ondangwa, they always came to inform me. This was how I managed to get a lift to the airport to collect our belongings. I brought them back to Odibo and sent a message to Kaino's relatives to come and collect her things. I remained at Odibo until her relatives had done so, then I sent a message to my uncle's homestead, telling them that I had returned and wanted them to come and collect me.

******

The next day, I received a message that a member of my family was at the office of the reception centre and had come to collect me. Oh, I was happy. As I walked to the office, I wondered who had come. Was it my sister? Or perhaps my brother? When I got there I saw that it was my cousin, Viitu yaHaimini, who had come for me. We greeted each other warmly. I then noticed that something was not quite right between us. My cousin was avoiding my eyes. He did not want to look at me. I was puzzled. Suddenly, he burst into tears and sobbed. Tears were rolling down his cheeks. It was all rather strange and confusing. I knew that, in my culture, people sometimes cry when they are overwhelmed with joy. Nevertheless, I did not understand my cousin's tears. Why had he greeted me with tears? I did not know how I was supposed to return his greeting. I could not just suddenly start crying too. How was I supposed to give back in kind, as was expected of me in this situation, according to tradition? I greeted him with a mixture of joy and compassion.

As a Namibian in exile, my life had been full of traumatic experiences that had hardened me in such a way that I did not cry easily. My life had required me to be the strong one. I was the one to console others, not the one to be consoled. My cousin had come for me as soon as he had received the message that I had returned. I knew people who waited in reception centres for many months for family members to collect them. I had waited only a day for my cousin to come for me. Yet here he was, crying. I just felt that it was a strange welcome. I waited for him to calm down and then I asked him, 'Ai, menhu wameme weya ngaa toxukaula ehodi, onawa tuu?' (My brother, you have come in a pool of tears. Is everything alright?)

My cousin replied, 'Many years ago, we heard that you had passed away in Angola, on your way into exile, in 1963. We held a vigil and a memorial service for you. People gathered and mourned you. We received condolences for your death. We were consoled, and consoled others. We made peace with it in our souls and accepted our loss. We buried you in our hearts and in our minds. When I heard that returnees had come home, I could not think of you because my mind had already accepted that we had lost you in 1963. I therefore did not make any effort to come and look for you.

'When a message reached me that you had returned to the motherland, that you were one of the comrades at the reception centre, I did not know what to make of the news. I came to find out what was really going on. When you walked in here and I looked at you, my heart started beating fast. I was filled with joy on seeing you return from the dead to real life. Indeed, it is you, alive! So many years we mourned. Today, we rejoice your return to life and your coming back home. I just wish our parents were here to witness this.'

As my cousin spoke, my thoughts went back to our life-threatening journey from Nambuangongo to the Congo, via Cabinda. And I, too, wondered how we had survived. I was shocked to hear that I was a dead woman walking. But considering all the dangers we had faced, I could imagine how people we had left behind might have assumed that we had languished and died. And, had we succeeded to get to the Congo, it must have been easy to imagine that we had been caught up in the political uprising there in 1964.[42]

My cousin accepted the reality of my presence, and took me away from the Odibo Reception Centre. He also informed me that my mother had passed away, as had my uncle and his wife, my aunt. Fortunately, the house was still in the hands of the family, as Viitu had bought the user rights to it. So we were indeed going home, to the place where I grew up. I was so grateful to him because he had received me well and with an open heart.

******

As we were walking out of the receiving centre, I heard my name being called, 'Mukwahepo, Mukwahepo!' A woman was running after me. I recognised her as one of the comrades who had been at the receiving centre when we arrived. She had spent weeks and weeks trying to locate

---

42 A reference to the Simba Rebellion of 1964, which began as a result of alleged abuses by the Congolese Central Government.

her relatives without any success. She was just staying at the reception centre because she had nowhere else to go. All efforts were being made to trace her relatives, but no one knew about them or where they could be found. This woman was running after me because she had heard that I was going home. When she caught up with me, she pleaded with me to take her and her four children to wherever I was going. Oh, this was extremely difficult for me.

I was about to be dependent on my family. I was bringing along my five children, and now there was the possibility of additional dependants. I knew nothing about my cousin's economic situation, or whether his household had the capacity to accommodate me, my children and these additional people. I realised, standing there, that I must have created the impression that it was in my family's blood to care for others. Despite all these questions and doubts in my mind, I knew deep in my heart that I could not turn my back on my comrade in need. The solidarity and comradeship amongst us returnees was still very strong. I knew that if I left this woman there, my conscience was going to punish me. As she pleaded, it became more and more clear to me that I could not leave her in that situation. I knew she needed my help. I felt duty bound to serve my country, my party and my people. We therefore took her and her four children along with us. Two of her children were small, while the other two were about fourteen and fifteen years old. People from the reception centre had heard her calling and had come to gather round us. Having listened to her story, some of them suggested that arrangements be made for her teenage children to go and board at the Odibo Secondary School.

And so it came to pass that my comrade, her children, my children and I left the Odibo Reception Centre and went to my cousin's house. This woman and her children lived with us for a year. As had been suggested, her teenagers went to the boarding school at Odibo and came home for weekends and during the school holidays. After a year of searching for her family in vain, she began to accept that all she had left of a family was herself and her four children. She started looking for land on which she could build a small house (*okaumbo*)⁴³. Then, one day, a nurse from our community who lived alone with her elderly mother approached her. She made her an offer to live with them on condition that she took care of her elderly mother who was too old to be left alone. The nurse worked at Oshakati Hospital, about sixty kilometres from our village. She had to live in Oshakati to enable her to fulfill her nursing duties, which included night shifts. My comrade accepted the nurse's offer. She lived happily with this family until 2003, when she too got a job.

My five children and I stayed with my cousin for six months after our arrival in Namibia. Then, all of a sudden, the biological parents of my children came to find me, one after the other. Some came just to tell me where they were living, and to say that they would come to fetch their children as soon as they had resettled properly. Although I was also facing the many challenges of resettling, the spirit which had guided our actions during the struggle was still very powerful within me. I thought of myself as the mother of all the motherless, and felt I had to struggle with the struggle children, whatever it took.

There was one child I was becoming concerned about, however, because no one had come forward to claim him. As I had never heard from his parents, it worried me that he might be an orphan. The parents of my other four children had written to me when I was at Kwanza-Sul, requesting me not to leave their children behind but to repatriate with them to Namibia. This boy's parents seemingly had never made any effort to look for him, even at the time of repatriation when all the parents were looking for their children. He had come into my care in 1976 when he was only a week old. I had looked after him, day and night, until he was fifteen years old. He was one of the children with whom I had travelled from Nyango to Kwanza-Sul. I was mother, father and grandmother to this child.

Six months after we arrived in Namibia, one of his paternal relatives visited me. He came to collect the boy in order to introduce him to his grandparents, then brought him back to me. This was a good thing and I

---

43 In Owambo culture it is usually a married man who owns a homestead, called *eumbo*. However, when a female owns one it is called *oka* (little) *umbo* (house), therefore *okaumbo*, meaning 'little house'.

was very happy because it was always my wish for these children to have a connection to their roots and close relationships with their families, if possible. Then, in 1991, his father's relatives came to fetch him again, and off they went with him. When I had not had word from them after a month, I went to find them and brought him back. But this situation did not last long as his biological mother arrived shortly afterwards.

His mother said that she had come to collect her child because his father's relatives wanted to honour him with *oshinyenye*.[44] Many of our children born in exile did not get this opportunity at birth to be bonded with their paternal clan, and had to receive this honour later, in their childhood or in their teenage years. There was, of course, no way I could refuse; to stand in the way of my child receiving such an honour would have gone against tradition and would have denied the child his ancestral blessings. The mother therefore took him, and I have never seen or heard from them since.

Things might have been different if this was to happen today. But in those days there were no cell phones. In fact, I did not have access to any telephone at all. I did not even have a postal address. All the information I received came to me via the SWAPO office in Ohangwena. However, I heard from other comrades that my boy had been taken by his father, who now lives with him somewhere in the city. I had looked after this child for the first fifteen years of his life. All those years, his parents had trusted me to be a grandmother to him, even though there was no biological relationship between us. Then they took him away from me and, to this day, have never looked back. This hurts. I am a human being. I love this boy. He was part of my life and then, suddenly, he was gone. I was left alone to deal with this.

Here is another story. The paternal relatives of one of my boys came to see me in 1993. They asked me whether they could take him with them, clearly intending to keep him for good. Then, about three weeks

---

44 *Oshinyenye*, meaning sweetness, is a special traditional necklace given to a baby by the paternal relatives. It signifies a bonding that unites the newborn baby spiritually with the paternal clan. It is special in that it is made from beads taken from the necklaces and waist beads worn by elders within the family of the child's father. *Oshinyenye* cannot be made from beads bought on the street. It usually consists of beads made from ostrich egg shells, river shells, copper beads, and a few *omusambe* and *onguluve* beads made from warthog tusks.

later, I heard a message on the Oshiwambo service of the radio requesting that I go and collect a child from the SWAPO office in Ohangwena. When I arrived there, I found the boy waiting for me. I did not ask him what had happened, but realised that things had probably not worked out smoothly between him and his relatives. I also realised that these children probably had difficulties living with new people, even though they were their blood relatives. All I said was that he was welcome, and we went home. I was disappointed that the relatives had returned him to the SWAPO office instead of bringing him back to me, in the same manner in which they had collected him. Then, at Christmas that same year, his father came to collect him from me again. He told me that this time he was taking his son for good, and that he would now look after him himself. I expected that the father and son would write me a letter to tell me where they lived. Days passed, and then the months turned into years. I never heard a single word from them. I learnt the hard way that the children I had once considered my own were out of my life for good, and that the relationship I had built up with them belonged to the past.

My other two children stayed with me until 2003. The girl had come to me in 1980, the year she was born. Her brother had also come to me soon after his birth, in 1982. The mother of these two children was like a real daughter to me. After our return home in 1989, she used to come to visit her children often and stayed with us for as long as she could. These children's parents had found it difficult to get jobs and were unemployed for several years after independence. Apart from this, they started going through a marital crisis that ended in divorce. The wife came to live with me after their divorce. This was helpful because the children were still in school. The boy was very bright and obtained excellent results, while the girl needed a lot of encouragement in this regard.

Although unemployed, the father of these two children tried hard to get money to pay for their school fees, uniforms and books. He was helpful. I could see how poverty was holding him back from fulfilling his fatherly role. He did not have a house of his own, but lived with his younger brother. I can tell you from experience that it is a crying shame for adults in our society not to have their own dwelling place. I could really feel his frustration when he said that he was tired of being a dependant. His younger brother was responsible for all his basic needs. His situation was unbearable to him.

I understood the situation of these comrades and, as long as they had no money to pay for their children's school fees, books and uniforms, I was glad to continue providing parental support and care for their children, as I had done in the SWAPO camps. The custody and care of these children had been entrusted to me by SWAPO. I felt that it was my duty to look after them. Although I had raised them at SWAPO's expense in the camps, there was no way I could have turned my back on them now that Namibia was free, and everybody had to fend for themselves. I had raised them from babyhood and they had formed part of my life. I just continued to live the struggle to survive with them inside Namibia.

In 2003, however, their parents finally found employment and their livelihood improved. As soon as they were in good financial and social standing, the mother came to ask me for custody of her children. I was left high and dry, and I was devastated. Today, I am cut off from their lives completely. This hurt is almost too painful to bear. At the time, some community members reminded me of the old saying, '*Kamukweni nande kappa efima lakula*'. (Even if you give the biggest share of the porridge to someone else's child, it will soon grow and realise who its mother is, and abandon you.)

The children whom I raised during the struggle, especially the two who remained with me until 2003, became the source of my inspiration. They gave me the energy and strength to live on. They gave me love and comfort. They never tried to run away from me and my poverty. They were part of me. I treasured them, and maybe also became too dependent on them as a source of family strength because, even though I love children so much, I never had a child of my own. So these children were a gift to me. If I had really wanted to, I could have looked for their relatives as soon as we had returned to Namibia, and sent them there. But I could not. I had raised them with a lot of love and care, and had watched them grow. I was the only parent they knew, and they looked to me as their grandmother, calling me '*Meekulu* Mukwahepo'. I had become so used to having them around me. I did not want a lonely life, and my children filled my life with meaning. I felt that this was my calling. I could never have given them away, or pushed the responsibility for them onto anyone else; besides, if they went away, my life would be empty. And yet, after independence, their parents and relatives took all of them away from me, and never looked back. It remained a disappointment to me, how the people who had left their children with me in exile while they went to study seemingly forgot about me completely once we had returned to Namibia. It was as if we had left behind our solidarity and comradeship in exile instead of bringing it along with us to Namibia when we returned home.

******

I had been staying at my cousin Viitu's house for eighteen months when my older sister, Maria, invited me to go and live with her. My sister was a single woman but had a homestead of her own at Onengali yaKaluvi. We discussed the matter with my cousin and he agreed that if we were sure that we would get along, as two independent adults living under one roof, he would support us. My cousin, a very wise person, reminded us of the old saying, '*Oiyuma ivali ihai wana kelimba limwe.*' (Two big clay pots do not fit in one room.) He asked us to be open with each other and think carefully about such a move. He advised us not to rush into it in the excitement of the idea of living together. I eventually did move into my sister's house, and always found Viitu's advise very useful.

While I was at my sister's homestead, her house caught fire and was virtually destroyed. My blankets and clothes and those of my children were burnt to ashes. All the things I had brought with me from Angola and Zambia were gone. This unfortunate incident left us in a situation of devastating poverty. I went to the SWAPO office in tears to ask for help. Luckily, the huge metal containers in which the personal belongings of the returnees had been brought to Namibia were standing empty outside the office. After listening to my problems, the SWAPO officials gave one of them to us in which to live.

I was very grateful. The only problem was that I had no way to transport the container to my sister's homestead. However, as an old saying in my mother tongue goes, 'God does not wean you like your mother.' As it happened, my old comrade from Kwanza-Sul, *Meme* Lydia Ndadi, heard about our misfortune and asked her son to help us to transport the container from the SWAPO office in Ohangwena to my sister's house at Onengali yaKaluvi. So, one day, while we were just sitting at home, we heard the sound of a vehicle coming towards my sister's place. Imagine my delight when I saw that the car was pulling my container! Our problems were solved. This container became our home for a long, long time. The SWAPO officials had also given me blankets and four metres of material. This was the kitenge material we had used while we were in exile. It had SWAPO prints on it. This special material reminded me of our spirit in the struggle. I therefore did not use it but kept it untouched.

It may sound strange to live in a container, especially in summer when it gets really hot and in winter when it is extremely cold. But our financial situation was bad, and we did not have the money to buy the corrugated iron sheets needed for roofing. Also, there is very little grass here in Namibia, unlike in Angola where grass is plentiful. I saw corrugated iron sheets in the shops but I just looked at it with my needy eyes because I had no money to buy it. I had returned to Namibia at an advanced age and could not easily get employment. It has been tough to live a life without a job and an income.

During this time, I tried to make contact with my older brother, Rafael, who lived near Omuthiya in the Oshikoto Region. When he did not come to see me, despite having sent him several letters and verbal messages, I decided to go and look for him. My sister accompanied me on this journey. When we found him and his family, we spent a week at his house before returning to Onengali yaKaluvi.

I was happy to find that my brother was doing well. I left his house with a good feeling and the expectation that he would return my visit. Yet the years passed by and he did not come to see my sister and I. He just remained quietly at his house. I felt totally let down. By not coming to welcome me when I returned to Namibia, I felt that my brother had rejected me and did not accept me any longer as part of his family. This made me appreciate my sister's offer to live with her in her house so that we could help one another in our old age. It made me feel loved, accepted and valued by her. Even though I had accepted her offer, I did so in the hope that I would find a place of my own one day. My sister's place was too small to support us both. The harvest from her mahangu field could not sustain us from one harvest to the next. It was hard to imagine that there was a person who was willing to accommodate another adult with her children in her homestead for an indefinite period. It was a rare generosity.

In 2000, my sister got ill. She did not respond to medical treatment and she passed away. I became her children's sole provider and supporter. I was the only aunt they had, and I simply took over her role and responsibilities. This is my situation today.

******

The 1989 election campaign was a remarkable phenomenon in our history. I was not prepared for it, at least not psychologically. It never crossed my mind that, after an armed liberation struggle, we would end up with an election campaign. In my opinion, this phenomenon was not fully understood by some of the political parties that were running for the election. Each political party used a different campaign strategy. This was confusing for the voters. Another major issue which seemed to confuse the voters was the names of two of the political parties running for the elections. The name of one party was SWAPO, while the other was SWAPO-D.[45] It puzzled me that the UN, which administered the elections, had allowed two political parties to register under almost the same name. Surely this would cause confusion, considering Namibia did not have a democratic voting tradition, and a high percentage of its population was illiterate.[46]

I also thought that some of the political parties were forcing their party onto the people during the campaign. Some campaigned as if they were buying voters, with their riches, their food and their drink. It seemed that the DTA,[47] for example, organised political rallies just

---

45 SWAPO Democrats.
46 The illiteracy rate was estimated to be over 60% at that time.
47 Democratic Turnhalle Alliance.

to *braai* (barbeque), eat and drink. Giving people food for free was the remarkable feature of their campaign. SWAPO had no money to feed its supporters at its rallies. I was worried about how our political party, SWAPO, would compete in this type of campaigning. How could it afford the expenditure of campaigning by feeding the electorate?

Although this type of campaigning came across to me as strange, it nevertheless attracted large crowds. I was relieved when I heard some people say, '*Ons eet by DTA maar ons stamp by SWAPO.* (We eat at DTA but we vote for SWAPO.) So, what appeared to be support for the DTA was merely people going to their rallies for the free food and drink. I thought that maybe this was what democracy was all about, but I doubted it. What we had been told by the UN in Angola at repatriation and what I was seeing in Namibia was like day and night.

I thought that what we needed in order to prepare ourselves for the elections was information. The voters needed to know the political standing of our political parties; what their political agenda was. What plans did they have for the country, and what would they do if they won the elections? The first political rally I attended in Namibia was a DTA rally. People were colourfully dressed in their party colours, waving DTA flags. Many wore DTA t-shirts and caps. Even their cars were decorated with DTA flags. I had never seen anything quite like it, but it reminded me of our Workers' Day celebrations. The only difference was that the DTA rallies were overly decorated.

Most of the DTA campaigners in our region behaved very militantly. Their cars, covered in party flags, were driven rather roughly. I was left wondering why, if an election campaign is a way for political parties to mobilise voters, their campaigners were scaring voters away with their rough behaviour. I was at our village cuca shop when the DTA campaigners suddenly arrived in their cars. When we heard them pulling up loudly and shouting their political slogans – such as Dee Dee Dee Dee, vote DTA for *okamuhaka* (sausage), *onyama* (meat) and the good life – the proprietor of the cuca shop told everyone to remain calm and to refrain from answering back. Many of us were wearing SWAPO t-shirts. When they saw this, they threatened to give us hell when they took over the government. They threw DTA t-shirts at us and said that we would be better off wearing them, because a SWAPO government would not even be able to afford to make the cool drinks we were drinking available in the country. They said SWAPO is from the bush and will feed us grass. Then they spun off in their cars, laughing loudly. And I was left wondering, 'Is this what it means to have an election campaign?'

Ten political parties took part in the first-ever democratic elections in Namibia in 1989. Every party campaigned very hard to be visible and to win votes. They did this by placing their party flags and posters on homes, shops, trees, poles along the side of the road; in fact, on any object where they would possibly attract people's attention. One day a political party would place its poster on the trunk of a tree along the road. The next morning, another political party would have placed a much bigger poster a bit higher up on the same tree. The election campaign ended up being very competitive, and sometimes confrontations broke out between campaigners from the various parties.

SWAPO and the DTA seemed to have been the main contestants. I did not hear or see much about the other parties. The South African officials and military troops who were still present in Namibia during the election campaign seemed to favour the DTA. Many of the Koevoet[48] members campaigned vigorously for the DTA. Although people addressing the DTA gatherings wore DTA colours, many of us could not make the distinction between members of the DTA, Koevoet, the SADF and the SWATF.[49] In addition to this, the DTA seemed to have a lot of money to support its election campaign. I remember one day when SWAPO had organised a rally at Oshakati and most people had to walk long distances to get there because the car-hire company that had originally agreed to rent its cars to SWAPO had let them down at the last minute. Apparently, the cars were in the garage, but the DTA had paid for all of them to remain parked. This apparently occurred throughout

---

48 Koevoet (Afrikaans for crowbar), also known as Operation K, was a paramilitary trained police counter insurgency unit in Namibia at the time. 'Crowbar' referred to Koevoet's mission of prying freedom fighters from the local population.
49 The South West African Territorial Force, was an auxiliary arm of the South African Defence Force (SADF), which comprised the armed forces of Namibia from 1977 to 1989.

the campaign, so SWAPO had to rely on its members' private cars to transport its supporters to its rallies.

Instead of informing voters about their political intentions, some of the parties opted for a dirty campaign by smearing and tarnishing SWAPO's name and image. Some of the allegations used against SWAPO were seemingly part of the apartheid regime's tactics to sway the election in favour of the DTA. It was claimed, for instance, that SWAPO was for Oshiwambo-speaking Namibians only. Yet there were people of all language groups in the SWAPO leadership. Another claim was that SWAPO came from the bush and was not capable of governing a country. People were urged not to allow SWAPO to come to power because it would apparently destroy the economy and infrastructure of the country. Some of these allegations were personal attacks directed against individual SWAPO members.

I know about these smear tactics because, although I did not go to all the rallies and campaign meetings, I listened to all the propaganda the SWABC was feeding to the public on the radio. My radio was on throughout the campaign, except when I went to bed. Despite the hostile campaign which targeted SWAPO under the leadership of Comrade Sam Nujoma, the party campaigned well and with honesty.

It was during the election campaign that I again met Dr Libertina Amathila. She had come to Ohangwena to address a SWAPO public meeting. She recognised me in the crowd and called out, 'Mukwahepo *ila-ila*!' (Mukwahepo, come, come!) This was truly great. We were happy to see each another again. I sat with her and her visiting delegation at the front row until the end of the meeting. I have not seen her since, except for in the media. She later became Namibia's Minister of Health and Social Services.

******

SWAPO received 57.33% of the vote in the election and was declared the winner. The party had worked hard and our people had voted wisely. Namibian independence was declared on 21 March 1990. SWAPO took over as the ruling party, and Comrade Sam Nujoma became the first

Namibian president. UNTAG[50] had played the crucial role of midwife in the process towards independence.

The date 21 March 1990 is one I shall never forget, even in my sleep. When we were repatriated from Angola to Namibia the previous year, we were all hoping for one thing and one thing only – for our party, SWAPO, to win the UN-supervised elections. It had happened, and Namibia was independent. We had all worked very hard, each in our own way, to ensure that SWAPO received the votes it deserved. And now there we were, in a free and independent Namibia, with SWAPO as the ruling party. This was a real dream come true.

---

50   The United Nations Transition Assistance Group, a UN peacekeeping force deployed in Namibia from April 1989 to March 1990 to monitor the peace process and elections.

8
LIFE IN INDEPENDENT NAMIBIA

In 1992, I was called to the SWAPO office at Ohangwena, where I was informed that I was one of a selected group of veterans to whom SWAPO was giving cattle. I was being given eleven head of cattle. My cattle were at a place called Mururani, where SWAPO had acquired a cattle post. I was further informed that it was my right to collect my cattle from the cattle post, but that I was equally welcome to leave them under the care of the SWAPO people at the cattle post, who would gladly look after them on my behalf. As I wanted to see my cattle, I went to Mururani to look at them with my own eyes.

I was pleasantly surprised by this wonderful news. In our culture, cattle is the most important asset to possess, the asset by which a person's economic standing is measured. If you do not have cattle in my society, you do not have any social and economic status and are treated almost like a child. I was therefore really very grateful that SWAPO had considered me as a beneficiary for these valuable animals.

I had to think about what to do with my cattle. I did not have land or a farm, nor did I have a cattle post. If I took my cattle away from the SWAPO cattle post, where would I take them? SWAPO had thought of me and had given me this gift without me having asked for it. I therefore decided to entrust my cattle to the care of my comrades and leave them at the SWAPO cattle post. The cattle were a great help to me.

Sadly, one of my children from exile who had returned with me to Namibia passed away in 1996. The ceremonial process around death in my culture must be observed, even under the most tragic or difficult circumstances. I was therefore confronted with a lot of mourners coming and going. The bereaved family is obliged to feed the mourners, who have come to share their grief and offer sympathy and solidarity. I realised that to fulfill this obligation I would have to fetch one of my cows. So, I walked to the SWAPO office at Ohangwena and asked for help to get a cow from the cattle post at Mururani. I was advised that it would be best to borrow a cow from someone in the community and repay that person later because it was a lengthy process to organise one from Mururani.

Eventually, I borrowed a cow from a neighbour and I gave my child a dignified funeral. After the mourning period was over, I made another effort through the SWAPO office to get to Mururani in order to fetch a cow so that I could repay my neighbour. In 1998, SWAPO took me to the cattle post. I was shown all my cows and felt truly grateful. I took seven animals with me. I returned again in 2004 and was happy to see that my animals had bred very nicely. I took six cows with me and left seven at the cattle post.

I was very content with this arrangement. After all, I did not have my own cattle post where I could have taken my animals and, in any case, was too old to hire people to maintain a cattle post for me. Besides, the cattle do not seem to do well in the Owambo environment. The seven cows that I took with me in 1998 all died in a rather strange way, and of the six animals I took in 2004, only two survived. The cows do not seem to like the weather in Owambo, so I preferred them to remain at Mururani. Although SWAPO does not update me regarding how my cattle are doing, I am readily given all the information I require whenever I go to the cattle post. I am perfectly happy with this arrangement and have no intention of changing it. This is also a question of trust. SWAPO has brought me this far, and I have faith in my party.

Following the declaration of independence, SWAPO set up its government structure. At the time of independence, I was jobless and without an income. The work I had done for SWAPO in exile came to an end on the day I was repatriated from Angola to Namibia. On my return home, I had in my possession my personal belongings and the five children whom I had taken care of on behalf of SWAPO in the camps in Zambia and Angola. Not only did I have no income, I survived each day as it came without knowing where my next meal would come from. This was the situation many of us returnees faced, yet it was soothed by the hopes of what independence would bring. In my mind, I started forming expectations of the new government.

I was hopeful that the comrades with whom I had been in the struggle and who were now part of the SWAPO-led government would remember me and give me a job. As I had done so well with the children in exile, I hoped to work in or run a government kindergarten. I still had hands and wanted to work for a living. I was confident that those of us who had spent our youth in the struggle and had returned home at an advanced age would be considered for employment. I had cleaned clinics, kindergartens and offices while I was in exile and would have been happy to do it again in Namibia. I thought that our government officials knew about the things that we had done during the struggle and would remember us after independence. Because if they did not, who else would?

I waited and waited but nothing happened. The day of my hopes and dreams never came. I realised that my expectations of independence had been based on a false dream. I saw that the comrades who were young and educated were getting all the jobs, both in government and in the other sectors. I was confronted with the reality of the Oshiwambo saying, '*Omajoka taadi mumwe nomifuwa.*' (When you separate snakes from rags, the snakes move on while the rags remain behind.) Many of the young people with whom I had been repatriated got jobs and moved away, while most of us who had aged in the struggle had limited job opportunities. My comrades with whom I had shared all the years in the struggle began to be separated from me, mostly due to poverty. Yet regardless of this harsh reality, I did not give up hope. I still thought the day would come for me to enjoy the fruits of our hard-won independence.

In 1997, seven years after independence, I turned sixty. I was still totally neglected and living under the shame of poverty. My thoughts ran away with me. I looked back, reflecting on how, in the refugee camps, SWAPO had looked after us so well, yet in an independent Namibia I was facing starvation. Some people told me to forget, to stop dreaming because I was now old. I was told that, in our country, one was disadvantaged if one was old, unlike in exile where everyone just worked despite their age. I was sixty years old, but I still had energy to work. Looking around me, I realised that I was not the only one in this situation. Most of my elderly comrades were being supported by their children. As I did not have children, I had to rely on other members of my family. This reality was difficult, but all I could do was face the facts.

It is hard to be an old woman and have to start a new life in a country where most of what we consume is bought with money. Life was painful, as I had no money and had to watch people having what I desired but could not afford. This experience was very hard to swallow. I was shocked by the harsh reality of life in independent Namibia. My mind became restless and kept going round and round, returning over and over again to my life in the struggle.

Then, one day, I realised that what I was experiencing was a direct result of what had happened while I was in exile. SWAPO had generously given its members the opportunity to study. Anyone who was willing and able to study was sent to school in various parts of the world. But I had never been offered this opportunity, especially in the 1960s when I was in Tanzania, probably because I had no basic educational foundation. So, the opportunities were gone. I was therefore illiterate when I left Namibia and illiterate when I returned home. Although I did undergo military training at Kongwa, I was never sent for further training abroad, maybe because the countries that trained SWAPO cadres had no facilities to train women. Also, unlike today, there were very few women in the military in those days.

Furthermore, at the time I did not strongly feel that I was missing out on anything by not going to school. I was content being at Kongwa, where during my training I felt I had an important role to play. I felt that the struggle was not only about formal education, but that the physical training and spiritual and moral education we were receiving were equally important. And later, when I became mother and grandmother to the children in the camps, I felt too that I was playing a truly important role.

I was always busy during my life in exile and I thought that the work I was doing would secure me a living after independence. I was serving my party and had no time to think about what was good for me as an individual. In the 1970s, when more young Namibians joined the struggle in exile, I became almost everyone's grandmother. Even people who were older than me called me *Meekulu* Mukwahepo. This was a sign of respect.

Eventually, I realised that these negative thoughts were breaking my spirit and draining my energy. I knew that in order to survive positively, I had to come to terms with my situation. We had fought for our independence, a fight that had cost both sweat and blood. People had died for our freedom. Yet I was alive, and fortunate enough to be living in a free and independent Namibia. Slowly, I made peace with my situation and moved on with my life. My one hope was to get a bit of land one day, to plant my mahangu and live on.

It was at Mururani in 1992 that I met Shikongo shaHangala again. He too had come there to receive his cattle from SWAPO. I could see that age was catching up with him, and perhaps he too had suffered from the reality of homecoming, resettlement and reintegration. He did not look well. That was the last time I saw him, and I never heard from him again. Recently, I received the sad news that he had passed away. I shall always remember him.

******

In 1995, SWAPO sent me an invitation to attend the celebration of Heroes Day at Omugulugwoombashe, where I was presented with a medal of honour. I felt good and I was proud. At this celebration, I met many comrades who were together with me in exile. I was very happy, and wished that the day and the ceremony would go on forever. However, as of course nothing lasts forever, the day came to an end and people departed for their homes. I too returned home to Onengali yaKaluvi with my medal of honour. My heart and soul was filled with the pride of recognition. Upon my return to my village, my fellow community members congratulated me for the recognition bestowed upon me by our SWAPO government. People greeted me with admiration and respect, saying 'Mukwahepo, you are a hero of our struggle.'

But when I got back to my container, although my children looked at me with joy – for their *meme* had been awarded a heroic medal – they were hungry and expected their hero to have brought them food. I had returned home with a shiny medal, but I still did not have anything to cook for my children. I was a recognised national hero with an empty stomach.

In 1991, I had registered with the government pension fund to receive a pension payout. Then, in 1995, not long after I was awarded my medal, I started receiving a monthly income of N$120, although it was only paid out every fourth month. The money helped, but was not enough to feed my household. I had to spend it carefully to ensure that my children and I survived on it for four long months. Whenever I received my pension money, I would immediately buy a large bag of mealie meal and a one kilogram bag of sugar. My household had to use this sparingly until the next payout.

Around 2000, this pension was increased to N$150 per month, and in 2004, it was again increased to N$1,000 per month. In addition to this, it began to be paid directly into my personal bank account. This was very good because I no longer had to face long queues at the pension payout points. In 2006, this pension was again increased to N$2,000 per month.

※※※※※※

During the struggle, we had fought hard for the liberation of our beloved country. We had fought with a strong belief that independence was coming. We had also believed that independence would bring everlasting peace and improved living conditions for every Namibian. But the reality was one of loss for me. After independence, I lost the livelihood I had whilst I had been in exile. I lost the children whom I had taken care of during the struggle. I lost the support of the exile community, which was no longer there because most people were reunited with their biological families.

So where was I in my life, fifteen years after independence? I did not have any income and had sunk deeper into poverty. I felt that I had been forgotten; thrown away in the dustbin of history by the very people with whom I had fought for freedom. Yet, the comrades with whom I was trained at Kongwa and with whom I lived at Nyango and Kwanza-Sul are my brothers and sisters. We belong to this big SWAPO family. You must understand that we had no one else to cry to, except to SWAPO of Namibia. SWAPO is my mother and father. I am a SWAPO person inside out. Even when I speak with sorrow or disappointment and you hear the disillusionment and hopelessness in my heart, you must remember that SWAPO raised me. SWAPO was both my mother and my father for all the twenty-five years I was in exile. Therefore, even today, whenever I hear someone criticising SWAPO I feel bad because I do not want my mother and father to be the target of negative criticism. It makes me feel as if I am also being attacked. This is how I feel. Even if SWAPO has let me down in something, it is difficult for me to talk about it to anyone because it is as if I am criticising myself.

And, naturally, the concept of comradeship disintegrated somewhat after independence, as our goal of the liberation of Namibia had been attained. People had to find new goals. Also, we were no longer living in the camps, where we ate the same food in the same kitchen, drew water from the same taps, clothed ourselves from the same store, and attended the same meetings every morning. In an independent Namibia, everyone had to look after themselves; to make their own home. The rules, livelihoods and activities of each person's home differ. The spirit of comradeship as we experienced it when we were living together in exile changed into the spirit of the individual struggle, at the household level, of people and their families.

Some of our comrades got good, well-paid jobs. Their income allowed them to afford comfortable lives. Others, like myself, have had to face many challenges as we have aged, and have not been able to do much about our living conditions. Many of the comrades with whom I was trained at Kongwa during the 1960s sacrificed their lives for the liberation of our country. A great number of them went to the battlefront and became military commanders. They led the war at the front, and many perished before Namibia attained its independence. I feel fortunate that God spared me to see Namibia becoming a nation and to live in an independent Namibia.

There is an old man who lives in our village, named *Tate* Shimbungu. He was arrested by the South African apartheid regime and jailed at

Robben Island for many, many years. Finally, he was released from prison just before independence. Since his release, he has been living with his relatives as a dependant under very appalling conditions. There are times when I have to avoid looking at him out of shame. Every time I see him, I become fearful. I think about my own poverty, and wonder how I will avoid sinking into the condition that he is in. I think about the pain I felt at being abandoned by the children I brought up, by their parents who turned their backs on me. Everyone knows *Tate* Shimbungu. Everyone worries about his condition. Yet if the people who know you well abandon you, who will pick you up and revive your spirit? Repatriation was easy. Reintegration has been extremely difficult, mainly because poverty has separated us from our own people. *Tate* Shimbungu, who suffered so much for our independence, I cannot bear to look at you, in your tattered clothes, begging for help. It makes me feel as if I am personally responsible.

As for those who lost their lives during the struggle, I cannot forget them although many seem to have been lost in our minds. Sometimes, I hear their names being mentioned in speeches by government officials, but not all of them, and not often enough to teach our young people that our independence did not come on a silver platter. When I look back and think about these fallen and too-often forgotten comrades, it makes me sad. Yet independence is my consolation. At least my comrades fought a winning battle. They did not die for nothing. As our national anthem says, their blood waters our freedom. But while we enjoy our freedom, we should always remember the bravery of those who fought and died for it.

When I look back to the 1990 period, the other thing I realise is that the beginning must have been very difficult for our government. Setting up a new government must have been a big challenge in the face of so many priorities that required resources. Our leaders had done well. Unfortunately, the living conditions of the elderly war veterans were not a priority, resulting in many of us being hard hit by poverty and helplessness. Although it has been difficult to go to bed hungry, I am comforted by the fact that our country is free. You can imagine my joy on the day the Veterans Act[51] was passed and implemented. I was sure that this would help to take care of me and my comrades who had been in the struggle, in the trenches, and in the prisons.

******

In 2006, I received the greatest honour and gift from the Namibian government. A two-bedroom house with a sitting room, kitchen and bathroom was built for me right here, at our village at Onengali yaKaluvi, just for me! The year 2006 will remain memorable for me. It was the year that I finally tasted the fruits of our independence. I was overwhelmed with joy to have been given a house, a shelter, a roof over my head by our government. I was so happy that I just sat down for a long, long time and cried.

This most welcome generosity came as a total and very pleasant surprise. I was not forewarned. People from a construction company just arrived at my sister's house one day, looking for me. They told me that the government had sent them to build a house for me. I could not believe what they had just said. Anyway, they started taking measurements and then left. Several weeks later, they brought all the building materials – bricks, cement, corrugated iron, and so on. They brought the workers and construction commenced. Oh, it was true after all! I just could not believe my eyes. My government had remembered me. I was extremely happy. I felt like I was touching the stars. Although I was reconciled in my mind to my situation, this came at a time when I thought I had been forgotten by society, and especially by my comrades with whom I had struggled for the independence of our beloved country.

The only unfortunate thing is that my house was built in the middle of an *oshana* (shallow depression), so when even the slightest amount of rain comes, we are swimming in water. It seems that the builders did not compact the soil and lay the foundations properly. They should have at least raised the level of the house to above the level of the *oshana*. In spite of this, I am a happy woman. I no longer have to live in a container. The Namibian government has taken me out of the shame of poverty. I have been given water on tap in my house and an additional outside

---

51 This Act was passed in 2008.

toilet. I have become a dignified hero of our independence struggle. I am living a new life, a proud and worthy life, like a normal human being.

The day the keys to my house were handed over to me by President Hifikepunye Pohamba, I nearly fainted from shock. I was so very grateful, because I knew so well by then that life can be a terribly difficult journey.

Then, one day in 2007, out of the blue sky came Prime Minister Nahas Angula. He just showed up on my doorstep. He had brought me a gift – some sofas for my sitting room. He delivered the sofas himself, and teased me about how old I looked. We had a good laugh, and then he left. Oh, I had no words. I went on my knees and thanked God for giving me people and a government and a party who remembered me after all, and who pulled me out of the shame of poverty and helplessness.

I also benefitted from the N$50,000 lump sum payment which was made to the veterans of the liberation struggle in 2011. With this very welcome additional support, I was able to buy household implements and to start some small-scale, income-generating activities to prepare myself to face old age.

I thank God I was not totally forgotten. Although it took a long time, assistance eventually did come. I will never forget the year 2006, when the comrades who are in our government remembered me and saved me from the ugliness of poverty. I am truly blessed. My tears are wiped. My government has remembered me and given me a roof over my head, and tap water in my house. I am forever truly grateful.

ABOUT THE AUTHOR

Ellen Ndeshi Namhila was born at Ondobe village in northern Namibia in 1963, and went into exile when she was twelve years old. She got her education in Namibia, Angola, Zambia, The Gambia, and Finland, obtaining an M.SSc. in Library and Information Science at the University of Tampere, Finland. She has worked as a researcher and librarian at the Multidisciplinary Research Centre; as a Deputy Director: Research, Information and Library Services at the Namibian Parliament; and as a Director of Namibia Library and Archives Service in the Ministry of Education. She is currently the University Librarian at the University of Namibia.

Ellen is author of: *The Price of Freedom*, her autobiography (1997); *Kahumba Kandola - Man and Myth: the Biography of a Barefoot Soldier* (2005); *Tears of Courage: Five Mothers Five Stories One Victory* (2009). She is currently a PhD student at the University of Tampere, Finland.

ACKNOWLEDGEMENTS

The Archives of Anti-Colonial Resistance and Liberation Struggle (AACRLS) for supporting the research work. Dr Zed Ngavirue and Commissioner Eliaser Haulyondjaba for reviewing the integrity of the initial manuscript under the AACRLS.

Tatekulu Mzee Simon Kaukungwa for the insights into Mukwahepo's life during the early years of the liberation struggle, especially in Kongwa.

My employers the Ministry of Education and the University of Namibia for supporting my writing in kind. UNAM Press, the reviewers, editors and all those who assisted in ways large and small to complete this book.

My husband Werner Hillebrecht for his unwavering support. My children, Monde, Mwalengwa and Ndadilepo.

www.ingramcontent.com/pod-product-compliance
Lightning Source LLC
Chambersburg PA
CBHW011713290426
44113CB00019B/2665